D0546338

Ellen White's World

A fascinating
look at
the times
in which
she lived

GEORGE R. KNIGHT

REVIEW AND HERALD® PUBLISHING ASSOCIATION
HAGERSTOWN, MD 21740

R&H Cataloging Service

Knight, George R.
    Ellen White's world.

    1. White, Ellen Gould Harmon, 1827-1915.   2. Seventh-day
Adventists—history.   3. United States—social life and customs.
4. United States—history.   5. Title.

ISBN 0-8280-1356-X

Contents

List of Abbreviations

AH	*The Adventist Home*
BC	*The Seventh-day Adventist Bible Commentary* (7 vols.)
Bio	*Ellen G. White*, by Arthur L. White (6 vols.)
CM	*Colporteur Ministry*
CT	*Counsels to Parents, Teachers, and Students*
CW	*Counsels to Writers and Editors*
DA	*The Desire of Ages*
Ed	*Education*
Ev	*Evangelism*
FE	*Fundamentals of Christian Education*
GC	*The Great Controversy*
LS	*Life Sketches of Ellen G. White*
MH	*The Ministry of Healing*
MM	*Medical Ministry*
MYP	*Messages to Young People*
PK	*Prophets and Kings*
PP	*Patriarchs and Prophets*
RH	*Review and Herald*
SC	*Steps to Christ*
SG	*Spiritual Gifts* (4 vols.)
SM	*Selected Messages* (3 books)
SW	*The Southern Work*
T	*Testimonies for the Church* (9 vols.)

A Word to the Reader

This book is the third in a series on Ellen White. *Meeting Ellen White* discussed her life, writings, and integrative themes, while *Reading Ellen White* covered principles for interpreting and applying her counsel. The present volume is a contextual study of the times in which she lived. The title, *Ellen White's World,* is a bit misleading, since the context in the post-Civil War years was radically different from that of the decades before the war. Thus it is more appropriate to talk of the *worlds* of Ellen White. The division of this book into two parts, the first dealing with the earlier period and the second with the postwar context, reflects that reality.

Ellen White's World seeks to portray as accurately as possible within the given space limitations the nature of the world that she lived in and the issues that were important at that time. In order to accomplish that task, a generous use of visual illustrations accompanies the verbal commentary. The present book provides an "airplane view" of its topic. Space was a constant enemy in the writing, even though it was a conscious decision to keep the volume short and thus in line with the series as a whole. But brevity meant that much had to be left out, including many of the finer points and nearly all nuanced distinctions. A volume of 400 or 500 pages would have allowed for more adequate treatment.

There are books similar to this one. The one that in many ways provided my model is Otto L. Bettmann's *The Good Old Days—They Were Terrible!* Bettmann's work, however, has more illustrations, makes little effort to integrate its various chapters within the philosophy of the times, and is not written for an audience with specifically Christian concerns. Another volume of a similar nature is *The World of Ellen White,* edited by Gary Land. The present book differs from Land's in its more extensive use of visuals, its integration of Ellen White's position on most topics in the text, its division between the pre- and post-Civil War worlds, and its attempt to set forth her worlds in a more integrated fashion than was possible in a series of topical essays by various authors.

Ellen White's World makes no attempt to provide information new to the scholarly world. On most topics and subtopics there already exist many book-length treatments. Thus the present work is largely a synthesis of historical scholarship for a general audience. Beyond that, it seeks to provide some interaction between Ellen White and her times.

I would like to express my appreciation to Tim Poirier, who suggested the idea for this book; to Bonnie Beres, who entered my handwritten manuscript into the computer; to Merlin Burt, Jerry Moon, James R. Nix, and Tim Poirier, who read the manuscript and offered suggestions for its improvement; to Gerald Wheeler and Jeannette R. Johnson for guiding the manuscript through the publication process; to Shirley Mulkern, Julius Nam, and Dave Sherwin for helping with the pictures; and to the administration of Andrews University for providing financial support and time for research and writing.

It is my prayer that this book will be a blessing to those who seek a more accurate understanding of the writings of Ellen G. White.

George R. Knight
Andrews University
Berrien Springs, Michigan

Dedication

Dedicated to

BONNIE BERES,
PATRICIA SALIBA,
and
JOYCE WERNER,

who have struggled throughout
the years to transform my
handwritten manuscripts into type.

Ellen White's World Before the Civil War

Part One

An early-nineteenth-century camp meeting

Chapter One

Millennial Visions

O n November 1, 1755, one of the most destructive earth-quakes in history up to that time instantly leveled the great city of Lisbon. As many as 60,000 people perished in a catastrophe that literally shook much of Europe, the Middle East, and Africa. It resulted in countless individuals turning their attention to the Bible prophecies relating to the second coming of Jesus. After all, hadn't Christ indicated that violent earthquakes would precede His advent?

Religious Millennialism

The Lisbon tragedy, however, offered but a mere foretaste of things to come. The 1790s would see the unprecedented up-heaval of the French Revolution. Its social and political eruptions reminded people of biblical descriptions of the end of the world. The violence and magnitude of the French disaster led many to examine anew the prophecies of Daniel and the Revelation.

Many Bible scholars developed an interest in the time prophecies and the year 1798. In February of that year Napoleon's general Louis-Alexandre Berthier had marched into Rome and dethroned Pope Pius VI. Thus 1798 for many stu-dents became the anchor point for correlating secular history

◄ R&H PUBLISHING ASSOCIATION

with Bible prophecy. Following the principle that in prophecy a day equals a year (Eze. 4:6; Num. 14:34), they saw the capture of the pope as the "deadly wound" of Revelation 13:3 and the fulfillment of the 1260-year/day prophecy of Daniel 7:25 and Revelation 12:6, 14, and 13:5.

At last, some suggested, the prophecy of Daniel 12:4 was being fulfilled. As never before, the eyes of Bible students literally ran "to and fro" over Daniel's prophecies as they sought a clearer understanding of end-time events. The late eighteenth and early nineteenth centuries witnessed an unprecedented number of books published on the Bible's apocalyptic prophecies. "Judging by the number of sermons, books, and pamphlets that addressed prophetic themes," writes the University of Notre Dame's Nathan Hatch, "the first generation of United States citizens may have lived in the shadow of Christ's second coming more intensely than any generation since."

A belief in the fulfillment of Daniel 12:4 and the unlocking of the 1260-year/day prophecy of Daniel 7:25 encouraged Bible students to continue their explorations. They soon came across the 2300-day prophecy of Daniel 8:14. LeRoy Froom has documented the fact that more than 65 expositors on four continents between 1800 and 1844 predicted that the 2300-year/day prophecy would be fulfilled between 1843 and 1847. However, while a general consensus existed on the time of the prophecy's fulfillment, opinions differed widely over the event to transpire at its conclusion.

Many saw the soon-coming event to be related to the beginning of the millennium. By the millennium they meant 1,000 years of earthly peace and plenty to be brought about through such means as social reform, national progress, and personal perfection. One of the nineteenth century's most powerful ideas was that human effort could bring about the millennial kingdom. Those holding to that view believed that Jesus would return *after* the 1,000 years ended.

Not all millennialists in the early nineteenth century arrived at their belief in the nearness of the millennial kingdom through a study of the time prophecies, but all had a sense of urgency. Thus Charles Finney, the greatest American evangelist of the second quarter of the century, noted in 1835 that "if the church will do her duty, the millennium may come in this country in three years."

In a similar vein the *Oberlin Evangelist,* in responding to the Millerite Adventists, claimed in 1843 that "the world is not growing worse but better" because of the efforts at reform being conducted by the churches and other reformers. Henry Cowles could write in like manner that "the golden age of our race is yet to come; . . . numerous indications of Providence seem to show that it may not be very distant." But, he hastened to add, "the event cannot take place . . . without appropriate human instrumentality [that is, reformatory work]. . . . The church therefore might have the millennium speedily if she would."

Not all Bible students agreed with the interpretation that Christ would come at the end of the 1,000 years (postmillennialism), however. Some held that He would arrive at the beginning of the 1,000 years (premillennialism). Foremost among those holding to the minority position in the 1830s and 1840s was a Baptist by the name of William Miller.

Like many other Bible students of his day, Miller believed that the end of the 2300 days and the beginning of the millennium would take place in the early 1840s. But he concluded that the cleansing of the sanctuary of Daniel 8:14 referred to the cleansing of the earth and the church by fire. Since Miller tied those events to the Second Advent, he concluded that Jesus would return "about the year 1843." Thus Miller was in harmony with many of his contemporaries that the millennial kingdom would soon appear, even though he differed with them as to the nature of that kingdom.

Miller was a logical and forceful preacher, and many began to gravitate to his views during the late 1830s and early 1840s. But Miller didn't stand alone. His most influential assistant was a pastor of the Christian Connection movement named Joshua V. Himes. Himes, as we shall see in chapter 5, turned out to be one of the public relations geniuses of the day.

Under the efforts of Miller and Himes tens of thousands adopted Miller's millennial views between 1839 and 1844. One of those converts would be a 12-year-old girl by the name of Ellen G. Harmon (Ellen G. White after 1846), who first heard Miller's message when he preached in her hometown of Portland, Maine, in March 1840. Ellen accepted Miller's position, and for the rest of her long life she lived with the doctrine of the nearness of the Second Advent at the center of her belief system.

SECULAR MILLENNIALISM

Not only was the religious world of the first half of the nineteenth century inundated with millennial expectancy; so was the secular world, albeit with different emphases and belief structures. Secular and religious millennial beliefs had intertwined in American thought ever since the beginning of the British settlement of North America. For example, we see the American sense of destiny reflected by the founders of the Puritan commonwealth of Massachusetts. "We shall be," proclaimed John Winthrop to his followers as they sailed to America, "as a city upon a hill. The eyes of all people are upon us."

The idea behind Winthrop's sermon is that the entire Puritan migration to the wilderness of North America was not merely to escape religious persecution but to set up the ideal civil community so that North American Puritanism could become an example to the world on how to establish the best possible of all societies. The Puritans really believed that if they did things right "the eyes of all people" would be upon them. Deeply embedded in that idea was the concept of covenant as portrayed in Deuteronomy 27-29. The basic idea undergirding the concept of covenant is that if God's people are faithful to Him and keep His laws, then He will bless them.

The "example to the world" and "covenant" concepts dominated Puritan thinking. Interestingly enough, those concepts maintained their prominence throughout the American Revolution and on into the first half of the nineteenth century. Thus even more secularized Americans came to have a sense of millennial destiny as they began to see their nation as "God's New Israel" and a "Redeemer Nation."

Even such deistic founders as Thomas Jefferson and Benjamin Franklin pictured the nation as God's new Israel. Upon being appointed to a committee to design a seal for the new nation, they proved to be much less deistic than one would have expected. Franklin proposed a portrayal of "Moses lifting his hand and the Red Sea dividing, with Pharaoh in his chariot being overwhelmed by the waters, and with a motto in great popular favor at the time, 'Rebellion to Tyrants Is Obedience to God.'" Jefferson suggested "a representation of the children of Israel in the wilderness, led by a cloud by day and a pillar of fire by night."

No one would speak more persistently of the American Israel's destiny than Jefferson. He wrote that "a just and solid republican government maintained here will be a standing monument and example for the aim and imitation of the people of other countries."

In the United States of the nineteenth century the more secularized millennial role for the nation as set forth by Jefferson and others always remained intertwined with more religious perspectives. Thus Lyman Beecher, a leading minister throughout the first half of the century, spoke for a broad spectrum of society in 1832 when he declared that the United States was "destined to lead the way in the moral and political emancipation of the world."

The concept of millennial destiny permeated the fabric of American thought and action in the period before the Civil War. In the eyes of the postmillennial majority, the recent political and technological advances had begun to provide the machinery for the creation of heaven on earth, with the United States leading the way. Undergirding such hope were the extremely positive evaluations of human nature and the concepts of the infinite perfectibility of humanity that the nineteenth century had inherited from the previous century's Enlightenment.

The great movements aimed at social reform (see chapter 3) and personal perfection (see chapter 4) that took place from the 1820s onward largely received their energy from the new nation's millennial vision. Tied to that vision also would be a continuing felt need to remain faithful to God as a covenant people. That idea would surface throughout the nineteenth century in such areas as Sunday laws and the concept of a Christian nation (see chapters 4, 7, 8).

Meanwhile, those who believed that Jesus would come at the beginning of the millennium rejected the view that humans could create heaven on earth through social reform and political experiments. They felt that only the coming of Jesus would solve earth's problems. Such was the faith of Ellen White.

Chapter Two

The Great Revival

As the newly created United States of America moved through the 1790s and the first quarter of the nineteenth century it faced two serious religious challenges. The first involved the challenge of deism, a skeptical belief that rejects Christianity with its miracles and supernatural revelation found in the Bible. Deism was on the cutting edge of ideas that would lead to secularism in the late nineteenth century.

Pre-Revolutionary deism was an elitist movement in America and as such didn't seem too threatening to the life and morals of the republic and its mission. But that would all change in the 1790s with the shocking atrocities of the deistically inspired French Revolution and the rise of a new popular deistic and anti-Christian literature, such as Thomas Paine's *Age of Reason* (1794).

The spread of aggressive "deistical societies" and the appearance of college students who called each other Rousseau and Voltaire now shocked Christian leaders. Many feared that the colleges themselves were becoming seedbeds of the skeptical new thought. Young William Miller, although not a college student, would be one of those carried away by the deistic enthusiasm of the age.

A second threat to the Christian mission of the new nation was the rapidly expanding West beyond the Appalachian Mountains. Many worried that people migrating away from the civilizing influence of the settled Eastern states would revert to "barbarism." To the religiously minded, frontier communities were unredeemed Sodoms. Thus Peter Cartwright could refer to his boyhood home in Kentucky in the 1790s as the abode of "murderers, horse thieves, highway robbers, and counterfeiters," and Lorenzo Dow could speak of the people of western New York as the "offscouring of the earth."

The Second Great Awakening

In the face of such threats the United States experienced the greatest religious revival in its history. One result was that between 1800 and 1850 the percentage of church members in the nation increased from between 5 and 10 percent to about 25 percent, while estimated church attendance grew from 40 to 75 percent. Beyond membership and attendance figures, Christianity saw a new birth in the life of the nation. One effect of that new birth was the Christian millennial drive inherent in many of the reforms that we will discuss in chapter 3.

By 1830 Alexis de Tocqueville, a noted French traveler, could proclaim in harmony with others that there was "no country in the whole world in which the Christian religion retains a greater influence over the souls of men than in America."

The Second Great Awakening, as the religious revival lasting from roughly 1790 to 1840 came to be called, did more than anything else to make America into a Christian nation. A generation of Americans turned away from the radicalism of the late 1790s and early nineteenth century toward the Christian faith. And, it is significant to note, most of them went not to a liberal form of Christianity but to a conservative evangelicalism that took the literal teachings of the Bible seriously.

Thus William Miller, who dated his return to Christianity to 1816, was not alone in his spiritual journey from deism to the Christian faith. The conversion of Adventism's founder took place in the context of a powerful awakening. That awakening also did much to mold the formative experiences of Ellen White and the other shapers of what would become Seventh-day Adventism between 1844 and 1861. Their world was a Christian one devoted to the Bible, expectant in millennial faith, and reforming in the social and personal realms.

The Second Great Awakening can be thought of as having three phases. The first took place between 1795 and 1810, largely in the unsettled West of Tennessee and Kentucky. The western phase of the Awakening gave rise to the camp meeting with its moving revivalistic sermons, enthusiastic singing, and powerful physical reactions among the worshipers. We will return to the camp meeting in our next section.

In the second phase of the Awakening the focus of revivalism shifted to the East, where such influential clergy as Lyman Beecher began preaching in revivalistic fashion in the northern Atlantic states. Such preaching did much to revitalize faith in the more settled areas of the nation. At the same time the eastern phase of revival began to move New England's theology away from the predestinarian beliefs of the Puritans toward a position more in harmony with free will and the effectiveness of human effort.

After 1825 the center of the Awakening would focus on Charles G. Finney, whose revivalistic success began in upstate New York but eventually spread to the great cities of the East, including New York, Boston, and Philadelphia. Finney, the Billy Graham of his day, is the father of modern evangelism.

Whereas one of the foremost revivalists of the Great Awakening in the 1730s claimed to have been "surprised" by the revival, Finney, in harmony with his less predestinarian theology, made revivalism into a science in the 1830s. "A revival of religion," he claimed, "is not a miracle. . . . There is nothing in religion beyond the ordinary powers of nature." Just as good farming was a matter of doing the right things, so was revivalism. The divine blessing usually came to the farmer who plowed and fertilized well. God's blessing combined with intelligent human effort was the secret of revivals. A revival could begin at any time if one

OBERLIN COLLEGE ARCHIVES

Charles Finney: the Billy Graham of the 1830s

used the right methods. Evangelists now substituted method for the Calvinistic predestination of the earlier awakening. The self-sufficiency of a frontier culture experienced with doing the impossible crept into revivalism. The farmer who merely sat down to await the results of God's predestined will would, suggested Finney, be in bad shape.

Central to Finney's success were his "new measures"—praying for people's conversion publicly by name, appointing a pew in front of the church as the "anxious bench" to which sinners could come as they struggled for heaven, the scandalous practice of allowing women to testify and pray in public before mixed male and female audiences, and the "protracted meeting." The protracted meeting was a townwide revival campaign that lasted for several weeks. In many ways the protracted meeting brought all the excitement of camp meeting to town.

By the late 1830s the revivalistic enthusiasm of the period between 1825 and 1835 began to wane. Beyond that, the panic of 1837 (an economic depression) and its continuing effects into the early 1840s had dampened the optimism of many Americans regarding the efficacy of human effort to bring about the millennial kingdom. Thus it is probably no accident that enthusiasm for William Miller's premillennial message took a giant step forward in 1838 and 1839. In the troubled world of the late 1830s Miller's teachings began to make sense to more people. People were looking for answers in both their personal and social worlds.

Perceived as a preacher with answers, Miller received an un-

ending stream of invitations to hold revivals during the la[te]
1830s and early 1840s in the churches of the evangelical denominations. Pastors found in William Miller a man who could revive
the sagging evangelistic thrust of the Second Great Awakening.
Thus several scholars of American religious history have seen
Millerism as the final segment of the Awakening. Everett Dick
has demonstrated that the maximum point in gains (of church
members in several denominations) occurred at the exact time
that Miller expected Christ's advent. And Richard Carwardine
notes that "in strictly statistical terms the peak of the Awakening
came in this adventist phase of 1843-44."

The Millerite crusade, therefore, should not be seen as a separate movement from the Second Great Awakening, but as an ex-
tension of it. As such, Dick is probably correct in his assessment
that "William Miller may justifiably be considered the greatest
evangelistic influence in the northeastern United States between
1840 and 1844." Ellen White would be one of his converts.

Unfortunately for Miller and his cause, however, most converts
made by Adventist preachers before mid-1842 probably converted
to general evangelical Christianity rather than Adventism's specific
premillennial doctrine. But that would change as Millerism ap-
proached its predicted end of the world in 1843/1844.

THE CAMP MEETING

As noted above, the camp meeting featured largely on the
frontier. Since much that happened at camp meeting was typical
of the evangelical religion of the common people for the first half
of the nineteenth century, we will spend some time on the topic.

The camp meeting had its birth in Logan County, Kentucky, in
1800. The most famous camp meeting of all took place the next
year at Cane Ridge, also in Kentucky. Scholars estimate the number
of attendees at 10,000 to 25,000. But even 10,000 was striking at a
date when the state's largest city had only 1,795 inhabitants.

The annual camp meeting for many rural Westerners was the
social event of the year. Whole families traveled as much as 100
miles to savor the camp meeting experience.

set the pattern for the early-nineteenth-century
One of the hallmarks of camp meetings was emo-
nt. James Finley, who was converted to a life of
Ridge, gives us a bit of insight into the dynam-
ics of the meeting. "The noise," he penned in his autobiography,
"was like the roar of Niagara. The vast sea of human beings
seemed to be agitated as if by a storm. I counted seven ministers,
all preaching at one time, some on stumps, others in wagons, and
one . . . was standing on a tree which had, in falling, lodged
against another. Some of the people were singing, others praying,
some crying for mercy in the most pitious accents, while others
were shouting most vociferously. . . . I felt as though I must fall
to the ground. A strange supernatural power seemed to pervade
the entire mass of minds there collected. . . . At one time I saw at
least five hundred swept down [i.e., 'slain in the Spirit'] in a mo-
ment, as if a battery of a thousand guns had been opened upon
them, and then immediately followed shrieks and shouts that
rent the very heavens."

The sermon stood at the center of the experience. Strong
preaching was the order of the day. To men and women used to
hard lives, mild homilies wouldn't do. The typical sermonic fare
consisted of vivid hellfire sermons contrasted with the happiness
and peace of salvation.

Frances Trollope, an Englishwoman who toured the United
States in 1827, gives us a view of such preaching. "The sermon,"
she noted, "had considerable eloquence, but of a frightful kind.
The preacher described, with ghastly minuteness, the last feeble
fainting moments of human life, and then the gradual progress of
decay after death, which he followed through every process up to
the last loathsome stage of decomposition. Suddenly changing
his tone . . . into the shrill voice of horror," he bent to gaze into
the pit of hell. Then the preacher told us "what he saw in the pit.
. . . No image that fire, flame, brimstone, molten lead, or red hot
pincers could supply" was left out, "with flesh, nerves, and
sinews" of the tormented one "quivering. . . . The perspiration
ran in streams from the face of the preacher; his eyes rolled, his

lips were covered with foam, and every feature had the deep expression of horror it would have borne, had he, in truth, been gazing at the scene he described."

By this time every face in the congregation looked "pale and horror-struck." Then a second preacher stood up "and began, in a sort of coaxing affectionate tone, to ask the congregation if what their dear brother had spoken had reached their hearts? Whether they would avoid the hell he had made them see? 'Come, then!' he continued, stretching out his arms toward them, 'come to us, and tell us so, and we will make you see Jesus, the dear gentle Jesus, who shall save you from it. But you must come to him! . . . This night you shall tell him that you are not ashamed of him, . . . we will clear the bench for anxious sinners to sit upon. Come, then! come to the anxious bench, and we will show you Jesus! Come! Come! Come!" This, of course, was merely the beginning of the emotional appeal as sinners wrestled with themselves on the very brink of eternal hell.

For early-nineteenth-century evangelicals, conversion followed a well-defined sequence of events. First, under the influence of a revival sermon a person felt a growing sense of guilt and wickedness. Then came the frightening awareness that hell was an entirely just punishment for such a wretch. Third, thus "broken down before the Lord," the sinner, stripped of pride and self-esteem, was ready to throw himself or herself on God's mercy. Next, if God had chosen the individual for salvation, he or she might experience a glimmer of hope and thus pass from being convicted and anxious to being hopeful. "Lastly," claims Bernard Weisberger, "he might have a climactic emotional experience, some special 'baptism of the Spirit,' some inward, unmistakable sign that pardon was extended and a crown of glory laid up for him in heaven."

Conversion experiences usually happened to individuals over an extended period of time, but when they took place for many simultaneously at such places as camp meeting a revival was under way.

Such was the revivalistic world in which Ellen White grew

up, even though most denominations had abandoned the camp meeting by the 1830s except for the Methodists, who had tamed them to a large extent by planning every detail and establishing firm regulations to govern unwanted religious enthusiasm. It was this tamer version of the camp meeting that Ellen Harmon knew as a girl, even though they were quite lively by twentieth-century standards. The Pentecostal spirit always lurked just below the surface in much of nineteenth-century religion.

While Ellen White responded positively to revivalism and the camp meeting throughout her life, she disagreed with the hellfire preaching of the day. Not only had fear of a vengeful God who tortured people in hellfire throughout the ceaseless ages of eternity plagued her in her younger years (LS 31, 49, 50), but she found the teaching to be unbiblical. She would later write that "it is beyond the power of the human mind to estimate the evil which has been wrought by the heresy of eternal torment." It was a concept that couldn't be harmonized with the love and goodness of God (GC 536). Many in her day had rejected the Bible altogether because of hellfire preaching. A case in point in the mid-nineteenth century were the Universalists, who went to the opposite extreme and taught that God would save everyone regardless of how they believed or lived. To Ellen White's way of thinking, the false views of God set forth in hellfire preaching had made "millions" into "skeptics and infidels" (GC 536).

Ellen White also responded negatively to the view that conversion was a well-defined process that climaxed in an ecstatic experience. Such an expectation had sent her into deep despondency in her youth because she couldn't claim that it had happened to her. But she did know that she loved Jesus, and she came in her early teens to know that God had accepted her and forgiven her sins. In response to what she believed to be a harmful teaching, she later wrote that "a person may not be able to tell the exact time or place, or trace all the chain of circumstances in the process of conversion; but this does not prove him to be unconverted" (SC 57).

THE REVIVAL AND MISSION

A wave of mission enthusiasm unparalleled in the history of Protestantism accompanied the Second Great Awakening. For the first time in their history the Protestant churches seemed to have fully grasped the magnitude of their responsibility to preach the gospel to all the world. The new enthusiasm for worldwide mission was multifaceted and extended throughout the nineteenth century and on into the early twentieth.

The era of modern missions began in England in 1793 when William Carey set sail for India. Then in 1795 the British Congregationalists established the London Missionary Society for the support of foreign missionaries.

A similar pattern developed in the United States. Enthusiasm for foreign mission first arose in 1806. Then in 1812 the first five American foreign missionaries sailed for India under the auspices of the American Board of Commissioners of Foreign Missions, founded in 1810. The American Board would be the first of many missionary-sending agencies to form early in the nineteenth century.

Foreign missions, however, were only the beginning of enthusiasm as the Protestant denominations sought to spread the Christian message. The American Bible Society organized in 1816, the American Sunday School Union in 1824, the American Tract Society in 1825, and the American Home Missionary Society in 1826. These and related societies were inspired by the millennial mission not only to take the gospel to all the earth but to make and keep America Christian. Mission consciousness in the nineteenth century permeated the American religious atmosphere to an unparalleled extent. The model structures and procedures set up by such religious outreach societies would help extend Millerism in the 1840s and subsequently Seventh-day Adventism. Mission consciousness was a vital part of the world of Ellen White.

Chapter Three

The Era of Reform

I t was a day of universal reform—a day when almost every man you met might draw a plan for a new society or a new government from his pocket; a day of infinite hope and infinite discontent," Henry Steele Commager wrote in the introduction to his book on American reform in the period leading up to the American Civil War in 1861.

The United States was awash with reforms of every type between 1820 and 1860. Fueled by secular enlightenment optimism on the infinite perfectibility of humanity, millennial visions of heaven on earth, and the distinctly religious Second Great Awakening, Americans challenged every aspect of their world. Whereas some reformers sought to change the structure of society through the establishment of communal utopias, others were willing to engineer reform within the existing structure. Central to the dynamics of the latter type of reform was the voluntary society.

THE VOLUNTARY SOCIETY

In chapter 2 we noted the missionary societies created to spread the Christian message to all the earth. Those mission, tract, and Bible societies were only the tip of an iceberg. Reform or voluntary societies arose in the early nineteenth century in almost every conceivable area of human interest. In the decades before the Civil War, campaigns for the abolition of slavery, war, and the use of alcohol became major factors in American culture. In addition, other societies promoted public education; better treatment of those who were deaf, blind, mentally incapacitated, or in prison; the equality of the sexes and the races; and so on. Beyond the social realm, one finds organizations sponsoring personal betterment in such areas as moral reform and health—including the American Vegetarian Society.

Religionists and secularists generally pooled their energies and resources in the hope of perfecting society through social and personal reform. Religionists, of course, went beyond their contemporaries through the establishment of strictly religious societies. The voluntary associations and the reforms they advocated existed not at the edge of American society, but at its very heart. It was an exuberant age in which people had a deep conviction that they could really transform their world. The evangelical Protestant majority believed that they must challenge and conquer anything that endangered the planting of the kingdom of God on American soil.

Hundreds of voluntary societies sprang up to focus their energies. The societies nearly always formed around a single interest. No one had to inquire as to the purpose of the American Antislavery Society or the Society for Promoting Manual Labor in Literary Institutions. The names expounded their purpose. But reform-minded individuals hardly ever belonged merely to one society. Reformers would "volunteer" to belong to as many as they had energy for. Being outside of denominational structures, the voluntary society allowed for cooperative action between various evangelical groups.

The special interests promulgated by the voluntary societies permeated the world in which Ellen White grew up and in which she spent her early adulthood. We will examine a few of the pre-Civil War reform issues most closely related to her interests.

HEALTH REFORM

C. P. Snow once wrote that "no one in his senses would choose to have been born in a previous age unless he could be certain that he would have been born into a prosperous family, that he would have enjoyed extremely good health, and that he could have accepted stoically the death of the majority of his children."

To put it bluntly, the good old days weren't nearly as good as nostalgia would make them. That was particularly true in the area of health. Average life expectancy at birth was 32 in 1800, 41 by 1850, 50 by 1900, and 67 by 1950. Currently life expectancy for women in the United States has reached about 79, even though it is somewhat lower for men.

Why the change? you might be thinking. The answer is fairly straightforward—better health habits, sanitation, and medical care.

The health habits of nearly everyone in the early nineteenth century left much to be desired. Not only did those with money gobble down large quantities of food at a rapid rate, but much of what they ate was unhealthful, consisting of a rich diet of meats, desserts, and highly spiced dishes, while fruits and vegetables were largely avoided by many who believed that the deadly cholera epidemic of 1832 had been brought about by fruit. Also many had suspicions that fresh fruits and vegetables were especially detrimental to children. The poor, of course, had more impoverished diets than the rich, but neither group had a knowledge of the basic elements of nutrition. On top of that problem, the food available was generally in poor condition because of lack of refrigeration and unsanitary processing. The result was poor health for individuals and epidemics for society at large.

Diet, of course, was merely a part of the personal health problem. Bathing habits, for example, also left much to be desired. Most people seldom took a bath, and some authorities claim that average Americans of the 1830s never took a bath during their entire life. Even as late as 1855 New York City had only 1,361 bathtubs for its 629,904 residents. And one would expect that ratio to be much higher than that of rural areas.

Sanitation was also a major problem in the early nineteenth century. Even genteel homes generally still had outdoor privies at midcentury. New York City had only 10,388 water closets in

A Philadelphia secondhand meat store

Diseased cows could hardly produce wholesome milk.

1855. Meanwhile, the seepage of massed privies made for some interesting bacteriological conditions in well water. As for garbage, Americans had no system for processing it. Most of it ended up in the street for the free-running hogs to root in. New York City of the 1840s had thousands of unchaperoned hogs to help care for the problem. Of course, the omnipresent horse droppings oozed in the generally unpaved streets in wet weather and were pulverized to highly flavored dust that blew everywhere in dry. And then there was spitting. In the days before the popu-

Citizens of New York City dodge herds of pigs at corner of Fourth and Broadway.

larity of the cigarette, Americans deposited chewing tobacco sputum everywhere, both inside and out, although the more sophisticated didn't spit on the table.

The lack of proper sanitation and health habits provided a fine formula for illness. But if you did get sick you certainly wouldn't want to go to a hospital. A trip there tended to be a death sentence in the era before the knowledge of germs. Epidemics were regular visitors to these unhygienic institutions originally founded for the poor. A hospital in the 1840s was a place of last resort—a place to go and die. People with funds didn't even go to a hospital. They had physicians treat them at home.

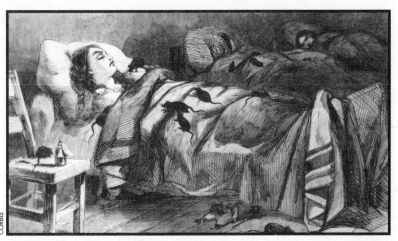

CORBIS

Hospitals: places where the poor went to die

Unfortunately, home medical practice wasn't all that sophisticated. The common view of disease was that the bodily "humors" must be out of balance. The cure was to rebalance them. A first step in that process often involved bleeding off some of the excess blood. Thus a physician over a period of days would drain a pint or two or more of blood from the patient's body. Purging the body generally followed the bloodletting. This was done through the administration of powerful drugs, such as calomel (from mercury) and strychnine, which we now know to be extremely poisonous. But in an age that believed that fever, diarrhea, and vomiting were symptoms of recovery, such drugs had the desired effect of rapidly and violently emptying the body of excess fluids. No wonder they called it the age of "heroic" medicine.

Surgery, meanwhile, was no less heroic when one considers it was done without anesthesia. Young Uriah Smith, future editor of the *Review and Herald,* experienced such a leg amputation on his family's kitchen table with his mother standing by to hold his hand. In the days before anesthesia speed was of the essence. It is said that army surgeons in the Civil War could lop off a leg in 40 seconds.

But even then the chance of survival wasn't all that great,

A satire of the surgery of the day, with coffins standing by to receive the results

since surgeons had no knowledge of germs or how infections spread. They did not feel any necessity to change aprons or knives or even wash their hands between surgeries, although they might wipe their knife across their soiled apron before beginning the next operation. Needless to say, early 1800s surgery restricted itself to amputations. Operations on the abdomen, skull, or chest were almost always fatal.

And what did it take to become a physician in those days? Not much. A person could go to a diploma mill for four to eight months to imbibe the medical "wisdom" of the day and then set up practice. It is little wonder that Oliver Wendell Holmes declared that "if the whole materia medica as now used could be sunk to the bottom of the sea, it would be all the better for mankind, and all the worse for the fishes."

It was into that context that we find the rise of the American health reformer in the 1830s. One of the most influential and representative was Sylvester Graham, who gained his opportunity to be heard in the wake of the first epidemic of the deadly Asiatic cholera in 1832.

We can catch a glimpse of Graham's ideas from an 1837 article in *The Graham Journal*. According to Graham, (1) "the chief food should be vegetables and fruit," (2) bread should be made of unrefined wheat, (3) "good cream may be used instead of butter," (4) food should be thoroughly chewed, (5) "flesh-meat and fish . . .

Sylvester Graham: a leading health reformer of the 1830s

had better be omitted," (6) one should avoid fat, rich gravies, and spicy condiments, (7) "all stimulants, of every sort and kind, as tea, coffee, wine, tobacco (in all its forms), cider, beer, etc., are prohibited," (8) "pure soft water" is the preferred drink, (9) "the last meal of the day should be light," taken three or four hours before going to bed, (10) *not a particle of food should be taken except at meals,*" (11) avoid eating too much, (12) "abstinence should always be preferred to taking medicine," (13) one should sleep about seven hours a day in rooms that have been "properly ventilated," (14) always avoid tight clothing, (15) "bathing [even daily] in warm or cold water is highly recommended," (16) "exercise in the open air is very necessary," and (17) "bread must not be eaten till 12 to 24 hours old."

Graham tied his regimen not only to individual health but also to that of the nation. After all, a healthy nation consists of healthy people. Health was the key to the future. Thus the Graham-inspired American Physiological Society could declare that "the millennium can never reasonably be expected to arrive, until those laws which God has implanted in the physical nature of man are, equally with his moral laws, universally known and obeyed."

To religious health reformers the laws of health were God's laws. Thus Theodore Dwight Weld could assert that "these are *God's* laws as really as 'Love the Lord with all thy heart' and 'Love thy neighbor as thy self.'" Obeying them meant a healthy body, while disobeying brought disease. The choice, Weld suggested, was "between *obeying God* and *resisting him, preserving life* and *destroying it, keeping* the *sixth commandment* and *committing suicide!*"

Closely related to the health reform movement and quite

compatible with it were certain forms of medical practice that opposed the drugging and bleeding techniques of the mainline medicine of the day. One of them, hydrotherapy, recommended internal and external applications of water as a therapeutic system. The water-cure physicians generally adopted the Graham system. Foremost among such practitioners were Dr. Russell T. Trall, who founded the Hygeio-Therapeutic College in 1857, and Dr. James Caleb Jackson, who established Our Home on the Hillside as a treatment center in Dansville, New York. Edson and Willie White eventually went to Trall's college for medical training and the elder Whites would spend several weeks at the Dansville water-cure institute in the 1860s when James was ill.

In summary, both the health reformers and the hydrotherapeutic physicians rejected the prevailing medical wisdom of the day. That was also true of other reform groups of physicians developing in the pre-Civil War years.

Those with a knowledge of Ellen White's counsels on health will recognize that she was in harmony with most of the reforming views of the health reformers. Thus she was in good company when she rejected the "use of poisonous drugs," "which, in the place of helping nature, paralyzes her powers" (MH 126; MM 224).

In a more positive line, Mrs. White harmonized with the reformers in her recommendation of natural remedies. "Pure air, sunlight, abstemiousness, rest, exercise, proper diet, the use of water, trust in divine power—these are the true remedies" (MH 127).

Also in line with the reformers of the day was Ellen White's belief that health reform had millennial implications. But she didn't believe that people could bring about the kingdom of God on earth. Rather, she claimed that health reform was to prepare people for the coming of the Lord. As such, it was "a part of the third angel's message" (1T 486). One of her contributions in the area of health was to integrate the message of health reform into Adventist theology.

The early Adventists were aware of both Ellen White's agreement with the health reformers of her day and her specifically Adventist contribution. Thus J. H. Waggoner could write in 1866 that "we do not profess to be pioneers in the general principles of the health reform. The facts on which this movement is based have been elaborated, in a great measure, by reformers, physicians, and writers on physiology and hygiene, and so may be found scattered through the land. But we do claim that by the method of God's choice [Ellen White's counsel] it has been more clearly and powerfully unfolded, and is thereby producing an effect which we could not have looked for from any other means.

"As mere physiological and hygienic truths, they might be studied by some at their leisure, and by others laid aside as of little consequence; but when placed on a level with the great truths of the third angel's message by the sanction and authority of God's Spirit, and so declared to be the means whereby a weak people may be made strong to overcome, and our diseased bodies cleansed and fitted for translation, then it comes to us as an essential part of present truth."

Before moving away from the topic of health reform, we need to take a brief look at a related aspect—dress reform. The female dress of the day aimed at producing a waspish waist. It accomplished that through armorlike whalebone corsets and unbearably tight lacing. The combination literally choked the vital organs and suppressed their natural function. The result was poor health and premature deaths. As if that weren't bad enough, heavy skirts and innumerable petticoats made a garment that dragged on the ground and often weighed up to 15 pounds. Skirt hems swept up the filth of horses and hogs along with disease-filled sputum.

Health reformers and feminists in the 1850s campaigned for a costume that would be warm and healthy. Some chose to don the reform dress popularized by Amelia Bloomer, which included a short overskirt that hung loosely from the shoulders over a pair of pajamalike trousers. As might be expected, many of those opting to wear bloomers also participated in radical feminist activities.

Ellen White once again argued for dress reform as a health issue. She not only counseled that women's clothing should be loose and light but that women should shorten their skirts eight

Women (with their heavy, wasp-waisted, floor-dragging dresses) were slaves to fashion.

or nine inches. Eventually she developed her own version of the health reform dress, but like other reformers she went back to more traditional (but not restrictive) garb when she found that her reform dress so distracted her audiences that they had a difficult time hearing what she considered to be her central message.

THE EARLY TEMPERANCE MOVEMENT

Closely related to health reform was the temperance movement. Before the 1820s few Americans, including clergy belonging

BAILEY, AMERICAN PAGEANT

Women's libbers of the day, in their bloomers. Note the public smoking and people making fun of them.

Ellen White in her version of the reform dress, about 1874

to conservative churches, saw anything wrong with drinking alcoholic beverages. In fact, drinking was a way of life for men, women, and even children. Some, of course, condemned drunkenness, but not the use of alcohol.

That would change in the 1820s as some began to see drinking as a central sin of the age and an impediment to civil and religious progress. A key person in waking up reformers on the topic was Lyman Beecher. In the fall of 1825 Beecher preached six powerful sermons on Intemperance. "Intemperance," he thundered, "is the sin of our land, . . . and if anything shall defeat the hopes of the world, which hang upon our [American] experiment in civil liberty, it is that river of fire, which is rolling through the land, destroying the vital air, and extending all around an atmosphere of death. . . . In our practice as a nation, there is something fundamentally wrong; and the remedy, like the evil, must be found in correct application of general principles. It must be a universal and national remedy. What then is this remedy? It is the banishment of ardent spirits from the list of lawful articles of commerce, by a correct and efficient public sentiment; such, as has turned slavery out of half of our land, and will yet expel it from the world."

Beecher's six sermons, published in 1826, were destined to

HARPER'S WEEKLY, 1874

Neighborhood bar. Note the drunk woman, the boy stealing handkerchief, and scantily clad children.

have a tremendous influence. One of the first and most important responses came from those who met at Boston on February 13, 1826, to establish the American Society for the Promotion of Temperance, known as the American Temperance Society. By 1835 the United States had between 5,000 and 8,000 local and regional temperance societies, most of them affiliated with the American Temperance Society.

The American Temperance Society preached against moderation and opted for total abstinence from all alcoholic beverages. By 1835 between 1 and 1.5 million people out of a population of 15 million had taken some sort of pledge to avoid alcohol. While some committed themselves to moderation, others took the "teetotal" pledge, which bound its signers to abstain from all alcohol.

The temperance movement broadened in the 1840s to include the Washingtonians, who aimed at working with the lower classes. But the major transformation of the temperance movement took place in the forties, when temperance proponents moved beyond moral persuasion to legislative reform. Ellen White's home state of Maine in 1851 would be the first state to legislate total abstinence. In the next few years at least nine other states enacted similar laws. Unfortunately for the reformers, most of those temperance laws were repealed or declared unconstitutional before the Civil War.

But the temperance movement was far from dead in 1865. It would revive again for a drive that would terminate in the Eighteenth Amendment to the United States Constitution (1919), prohibiting the manufacture, sale, or use of all alcoholic beverages. Ellen White would become a sought-after speaker in the movement's post-Civil War phase.

EDUCATIONAL REFORM

"Education, then, beyond all other devices of human origin, is the great equalizer of the conditions of men. . . . It gives each man the independence and the means by which he can resist the selfishness of other men. It does better than to disarm the poor of their hostility towards the rich: it prevents being poor. . . . If this educa-

New York ghetto school

tion should be universal and complete, it would do more than all things else to obliterate factitious distinctions in society."

Thus wrote Horace Mann in 1848, the nation's foremost and most successful reformer in the prolonged battle to provide quality universal elementary education in Massachusetts. He expressed a faith in the power of education that had grown out of eighteenth-century French thought regarding the intrinsic goodness of human nature. If people were good by nature, then universal education could transform them and the entire world. Many viewed education as an unlimited tool for human enrichment as visionaries sought to move the world toward social perfection.

But schooling had a long way to go in the pre-Civil War years if it was to be effective. For one thing, the nation had few public elementary schools. Then again, all types of public and most private schools suffered from a lack of quality. Instruction largely involved rote memorization. Students packed into rooms without proper ventilation, desks, or lighting. Teachers had few qualifications, and school boards often hired them for their physical ability to control students rather than their teaching talent. Instructional materials were primitive at best.

As if those problems were not enough, sanitary conditions at school were deplorable, a problem illuminated by the plea of one schoolteacher for the installation of outdoor privies. Her school board advised her that "there were plenty of trees in the yard to get behind." It also denied her suggestion that the single well-dipper be replaced with more hygienic individual cups as being "undemocratic." No wonder Mann's contemporaries could complain of "schoolhouses being not only dangerous to the health of children but as being actually a cause of death to some of them."

Against such abuses Mann and his fellow reformers fought with great vigor. They sought to reshape every aspect of the schools. At the top of their list was the need to provide more healthful facilities and an adequate knowledge of physiology and hygiene.

Religion was pervasive in elementary education before the Civil War. Even the public schools of the period taught religion, albeit not a sectarian variety. Rather, they taught a generic Protestantism consisting of those beliefs held in common by the nation's leading denominations. As such the schools helped keep America Protestant. Roman Catholics, as we might expect, were not overjoyed with such offerings. As a result, in the 1840s they began their own parochial system.

Secondary and collegiate education was the realm of the elite and the classical languages (Greek and Latin), classical literature, higher mathematics, morals, religion, and a smattering of natural philosophy dominated their curriculums. But by the early 1830s some institutions of higher learning were ready to go their own way. In 1831, for example, the Society for Promoting Manual Labor in Literary Institutions formed, with Theodore Dwight Weld as its general agent. The society's founders had the conviction "that a reform in our seminaries of learning was greatly needed, both for the preservation of health and in giving energy to the character by habits of vigorous and useful exercise."

One of the most influential schools in the movement for manual labor, or vocational education, in literary institutions was Oberlin College in northeastern Ohio. Oberlin's founder wrote in 1833 that "the system of education in this Institute will provide for the *body and heart* as well as the *intellects;* for it aims at the best education of the *whole man."* Oberlin's founders left no doubt in anyone's mind that the institution existed to help usher in the millennium through evangelism and moral reform.

Part of the Oberlin reform involved destroying the monopolistic hold of the classics on the curriculum. The school's president proclaimed that the Greek and Roman writings were "better adapted to educate heathen . . . than Christians. He be-

Oberlin College campus in 1846

Oberlin College seal, with learning and labor
motto and students working in fields

lieved the mind could be disciplined as well by the study of
Hebrew and Greek Scriptures. . . . He would fill their minds
with truth, facts, practical, available knowledge." Thus the
Oberlin reformers not only downplayed the classics but uplifted
the curricular role of the Bible.

More radical than Oberlin's attack on the classics was its emphasis on the physical and practical side of education. The school's
First Annual Report claimed that the Manual Labor Department "is
considered *indispensable* to a complete education." The document
offered several reasons to buttress its assertion. First, manual labor
would "preserve the student's health." Thus the school required

all students to labor daily. Second, "there being an intimate sympathy between soul and body, their labor promotes . . . clear and strong thought with a happy moral temperament."

Third, the manual labor system offered financial advantages. "For while taking that exercise necessary to health, a considerable portion of the student's expense may be defrayed." Fourth, the program aided "in forming habits of industry and economy." Last, the system provided an acquaintance with the common things of daily life. "In a word, it meets the wants of man as a *compound* being, and prevents the common and amazing waste of money, time, health, and life."

Ellen White, as in most areas of reform, tended to be in agreement with the reforms set forth by Mann and the Oberlinites. For example, she also argued for the education of the whole person, including "the physical, the mental, and the spiritual powers" (Ed 13); she uplifted the benefits of manual labor; she highlighted the need for healthier classrooms, curricula that challenged thought, and better teachers; she argued that "a knowledge of physiology and hygiene should be the basis of all educational effort" (Ed 195), since all that people hoped to accomplish depended on their health; and she also, in agreement with the Oberlinites, set forth the need to substitute the Bible for the classics as the center of the curriculum.

But Ellen White did not merely repeat the counsel of the educational reformers; she moved beyond them in placing the role of education within the pattern of the great controversy. Thus, for her, education meant "more than a preparation for the life that now is. It has to do with the whole being, and with the whole period of existence possible to man" (Ed 13). More specifically, she packaged her educational philosophy in terms of the Genesis fall and our restoration in Christ. The teacher's primary aim was to lead young people to Jesus. Thus she equated education with redemption, "the great object of life" (Ed 14-16, 29, 30).

THE MOVEMENT TO FREE THE SLAVES
The movement to do away with slavery became a progres-

sively dominant factor in American life, one that led the nation into a bloody civil war lasting from 1861 to 1865. The demand for immediate emancipation of all slaves arose in the 1830s, primarily as a result of the Second Great Awakening. The revivalism of the 1820s and 1830s stressed repentance from all sin, and many perceived slavery as a sin. By 1833 such religiously inspired leaders as William Lloyd Garrison and Theodore Dwight Weld linked up with others to form the American Antislavery Society. Several of the foremost Millerites (including Joshua Himes, George Storrs, and Charles Fitch) prominently participated in the antislavery struggle. The American Antislavery Society was quite unpopular even in the North during its early years, but by the late 1830s it had gained wider acceptance.

What had been a festering problem in the 1830s became an explosive issue in the 1840s. It progressively polarized both the nation and the churches. The Methodists, for example, divided into northern and southern denominations in 1844, and the Baptists followed suit a year later. The political realm witnessed the rise of the Liberty Party with James G. Birney as its presidential candidate in 1840 and 1844. By 1848 it had combined with the Free Soil Party. Neither party got many votes, but by holding the balance of power they shifted the course of national politics in the elections of 1844 and 1848.

By the 1850s the slavery issue had reached crisis proportions. A series of individual crises over slavery hit the nation in the fifties, but none proved to be more divisive than the Fugitive Slave Act of 1850. That act made Northerners directly responsible for helping recapture escaped slaves who had fled the South. The legislation imposed heavy penalties on those who refused to aid government slave catchers or who obstructed recapture. Beyond that, those accused of being fugitives but were actually free Blacks lost the right of trial by jury, and courts would not admit their testimony as evidence when their cases went to trial.

The Fugitive Slave Act set the stage for civil disobedience by those who were morally outraged at what they believed to be an unconstitutional and unchristian enactment. As noted earlier, slav-

Slave traders' advertisement. Figures of running slaves were often used in advertising for runaways.

ery and related issues led in the 1860s to America's bloodiest war, with more lives lost than in all other American wars combined.

As we might expect, being the reformer that she was, Ellen White stood firmly against slavery and saw it as a moral issue. In the midst of the Civil War she agreed with the radical abolitionists that God was punishing the "South for the sin of slavery, and the North for so long suffering its overreaching and overbearing influence" (1T 264). Beyond that, she went so far as to advocate civil disobedience to the Fugitive Slave Act. "When the laws of men conflict with the word and law of God, we are to obey the latter. . . . The law of our land requiring us to deliver a slave to

his master, we are not to obey; and we must abide the consequences of violating this law. The slave is not the property of any
man. God is his rightful master, and man has no right to take
God's workmanship into his hands, and claim him as his own"
(1T 201, 202).

THE ROLE OF WOMEN

Early in the nineteenth century women had only a slim place
in society outside the home. For example, they had no right to
vote, college education was unavailable to them, and married
women didn't have the right to hold property, even property
they brought into the marriage. They were voiceless not only in
society, but also in the church. Finney, for example, created quite
a scandal when he allowed females to testify publicly before
mixed audiences of men and women.

The status of women would slowly begin to change in the era
of reform. Oberlin College, a radical and reformatory institution,
opened its doors to females in the 1830s, and between 1836 and
1850 most states enacted some form of legislation on the right of
married women to own property.

But the largest impulse toward women's rights came in connection with the antislavery movement. In the late 1830s some
of the more radical abolitionists, such as Garrison, had permitted
women to speak to mixed assemblies, and in 1838 Garrison's
New England Antislavery Society accepted women as members.
By 1840 the "woman question" split the abolitionist movement.
Undergirding the split was the larger philosophical issue of
whether abolitionists should challenge all unjust structures or
merely slavery.

Meanwhile the "woman question" within slavery blossomed
into a full-blown movement for women's rights in the 1840s.
Women schooled in reform ideology applied what they knew
about the restricted condition of slaves to their own situation. In
1848 reformers led by Lucretia Mott and Elizabeth Cady Stanton
(both antislavery advocates) sponsored a women's rights convention in Seneca Falls, New York. At that meeting we find the

genesis of a women's rights movement that would extend throughout the balance of the century and into the twentieth.

The "woman question" is important in studying the world of Ellen White because she was a woman in a man's world. She was not only a woman who began to speak to mixed audiences in 1845 but also an activist who recommended better education for women. Furthermore, she eventually became a noted speaker not only among Adventists but in the larger world of temperance rallies.

It should be recognized, however, that Mrs. White came from Methodism, the sector of evangelical Protestantism most favorable to the public role of females in mixed audiences. In 1853 Luther Lee of the Wesleyan Methodists preached the ordination sermon for Antoinette D. Brown, a graduate of Oberlin and probably the first woman to be fully ordained to the Christian ministry in an American denomination. And in the early 1840s Phoebe Palmer, who had no interest in ordination, began to defend women's rights to preach on the basis of the gift of the Spirit to the church at Pentecost, with its promise that "your sons and your daughters shall prophesy." Mrs. Palmer belonged to the same branch of Methodism as Ellen White.

Chapter Four

Religious Impulses

The early-nineteenth-century social ferment in the United States not only was empowered by millennial expectations and energized by revivals and reform, but was perhaps the most fruitful period in world history for the development of new Christian movements. The reason for that prolific situation harks back to the Revolutionary period and especially to the First Amendment to the United States Constitution, which provides for the separation of church and state. In previous societies, both ancient and modern, the two had always been united, with the state officially sponsoring one religious group. In Christian nations the official group became the church, while all minority religious groups were thought of as sects that to one degree or another lost some or all of their religious liberty and who often endured persecution.

That changed in the new nation in which no one Christian group could gain national dominance. The result was a free market economy in religious affairs that regarded all Christian groups as equal in legal standing. Thus the early United States gave birth to a new religious entity called the denomination, with the government defining no one denomination as special or better. To the contrary, each denomination could survive only as it could "sell" its product in the open marketplace. Those denominations that appealed to the people were the ones that grew.

The opening up of legal equality for all Christian groups led to a religious experimentation unparalleled in history. Some of the experiments were quite orthodox in terms of traditional Christian doctrines, and some we might best define as unique. As Philip Schaff put it in 1844: "Tendencies, which had found no political room to unfold themselves in other lands, wrought here [the United States] without restraint. . . . Every theological vagabond and peddler may drive here his bungling trade, without passport or license, and sell his false ware at pleasure. What is to come of such confusion is not now to be seen." This chapter will examine some of the most influential religious impulses in early-nineteenth-century America.

THE RISE OF THE "DEMOCRATIC" CHURCHES

The more aristocratic Episcopalians and Congregationalists and the somewhat less prestigious Presbyterians had numerically and politically dominated the religious affairs of the Colonial period of American history. They were the powerful churches, but that would drastically change in the early nineteenth century. The first half of the century would see the rise of the people's churches—especially the Methodists and Baptists.

Those two denominations were particularly suited for reaching the common people and for moving forward with an ever-expanding frontier. Whereas the churches that had dominated the Colonial era expected a formally educated clergy, the Methodists and Baptists were willing to use lay preachers and preachers who had read their way into theology while serving as apprentices to more experienced ministers. That was important, since, as Winthrop Hudson points out, "the future in America—numerically speaking—belonged to those groups which could provide an ample supply of ministerial leadership."

The genius of Methodism was the "circuit system," in which one pastor served a number of churches and visited them periodically in the course of riding the circuit. When new opportuni-

HARPER'S WEEKLY

The circuit rider was a familiar figure on the frontier.

ties arose, the pastor just added new companies to the route until the circuit needed to split in two. Meanwhile the nurturing of the flocks largely rested in the hands of local lay preachers or class leaders.

The Baptists also had a system that succeeded in frontier conditions. Like the Methodists, the early Baptists put little stock in a formally educated clergy. While their ministers generally served one church, they did so on a part-time basis. Since they often received a small salary or no salary at all, they made their way as farmers or mechanics and lived close to the congregation they served. Given the fact that any group of like-minded individuals could form a Baptist church and call a minister (often from their own midst), the Baptists were well adapted to expand as the nation moved across the continent.

Denominations that used only college-and seminary-trained pastors had no way of keeping up with the Baptists and Methodists. Beyond that, their pastors were often out of touch with the common people of rural America at a time when the country was nearly all rural.

As a result, the Baptists and Methodists each went from about 2,700 congregations in 1820 to 12,150 and 19,883, respectively, in 1860, while the Congregationalists and Episcopalians increased only from 1,100 to 2,234 and 600 to 2,145 churches, respectively, in the same period. By midcentury the Baptists and the Methodists would be by far the largest Protestant denominations in America, even though nobody could have predicted their dominance at the time of the American Revolution in 1776. It was truly a century for the expansion of the common people's religion.

RESTORATIONISM AND BACK TO THE BIBLE

Closely related to the rise of Methodism and the Baptists with their democratic impulses was the restorationist movement. In essence, restorationism centered on a drive to get back to the Christianity of the New Testament. That meant rejecting the creeds that had bound men and women to esoteric doctrines that some believed were nothing more than the speculations of so-called learned men. Thus the restorationist movement rejected not only creeds but also the authority of the clergy.

A new generation of Christians demanded, in the light of the American Revolution, a church founded on democratic principles and the right of the common people to interpret the New Testament for themselves. They called for a religion of the people, by the people, and for the people.

The central figures in this early-nineteenth-century reform movement were Elias Smith (a Baptist), James O'Kelly (a Methodist), Barton Stone (a Presbyterian), Alexander Campbell (a Presbyterian), and Abner Jones (a Baptist). The general consensus of all five men, working independently from each other, was that the Reformation had not been completed and would not be until the church got back to a plain reading of the New Testament. In Campbell's words: "Just in so far as the ancient order of things, or the religion of the New Testament, is restored, just so far has the Millennium commenced."

"No creed but the Bible" was the call of the restorationist movement. As John Rogers put it: "As soon as she [the church] established a human creed as a test of truth and union, she made rapid strides into Babylon . . . : The Man of Sin and Son of Perdition was soon revealed, and seen clambering into the temple of God . . . ; [then] the reign of priestly terror began." The only safety, wrote Campbell, is to go to the Bible for every aspect of God's will. One must move beyond the perversions of eighteen centuries of Christian theology and priestcraft and get back to the Word of God. "I have endeavored," he penned, "to read the Scriptures as though no one had read them before me. . . . I am against being influenced by any foreign name, authority, or system whatever."

The priesthood of believers and private interpretation of the Bible formed the core of the restorationist movement. For the restorationists those concepts stood at the center of "Gospel liberty."

Restorationism, along with Methodism and the Baptist movement, is important in understanding Adventism. After all, James White and Joseph Bates (two of the three founders of Seventh-day Adventism) were restorationists, as was Joshua V. Himes (the second most influential Millerite Adventist). And William Miller was a Baptist, while Ellen White was a Methodist.

It is no accident that early Adventists claimed that they had "no creed but the Bible" or that William Miller could state that those who studied the Bible in faith could trust that they would arrive at truth even "though they may not understand Hebrew or Greek." These were motifs at the very core of the democratic Christianity that arose in early-nineteenth-century America. The same is true of Miller's counsel to a young pastor when he said: "You must preach *Bible,* you must prove all things by *Bible,* you must talk *Bible,* you must exhort *Bible,* you must pray *Bible,* and love *Bible,* and do all in your power to make others love *Bible* too."

We should also recognize that the concepts of the primacy of Scripture and the restorationist view of history stand at the very heart of Ellen White's *Great Controversy.* To her the Reformation was not something that happened in the sixteenth century but a line of continual advancement as God sought to lead His people back to the great truths of the Bible. Early Adventists such as Joseph Bates also saw the Sabbath in terms of restorationism. The seventh-day Sabbath, he claimed, was one of those truths that needed to be restored to the church before the coming of Jesus.

THE DRIVE TOWARD PERFECTION

Timothy Smith correctly notes that Christian perfection is "one of the nineteenth century's most persistent and socially significant themes" and that "the hunger for holiness lay near the heart of every movement concerned with developing a more meaningful Christianity."

The modern Protestant teachings on perfection find their roots in the theology of John Wesley, the founder of Methodism. Wesley did not equate perfection with absolutely perfect performance or what we might think of as absolute sinlessness. To the contrary, Wesley defined perfection as "pure love reigning alone in the heart and life." Again he penned that perfection "is purity of intention, dedicating all the life to God. It is the giving God all our heart. . . . It is the devoting, not a part, but all, our soul, body, and substance, to God. In another view, it is all the mind which was in Christ, enabling us to walk as Christ walked. It is the circumcision of the heart from all filthiness, all inward as well as outward pollution. It is a renewal of the heart in the whole image of God, the full likeness of Him that created it. In yet another, it is . . . loving God with all our heart, and our neighbour as ourselves."

Wesley taught that perfection came about as a second act of grace that God instantly worked in the believer's life. He also thought that Christians could be conscious of their own perfection.

The early Methodists brought Wesley's concepts of perfection with them to America. The 1840s and 1850s witnessed a renewed interest in the topic in American Christianity both within and outside of Methodism. Especially important within Methodism was the work of Phoebe Palmer.

Ellen White, who grew up in the Wesleyan tradition, espoused essentially the same definition of perfection as Wesley. That is made clear in such passages as *Christ's Object Lessons,* page 69, where she talks about perfectly reproducing the character of Christ before He comes again. In the previous two pages she demonstrates her affinity with Wesley's definition of perfection, as opposed to the medieval monastic sinless concept of perfection, when she equates character perfection with perfect love and the unselfish spirit of Christ.

Mrs. White, however, did not agree with all of Wesley's teachings on perfection. For example, she flatly denied his view of an "instantaneous" second work. Likewise, she rejected the idea that Christians would be conscious of their perfection.

The surprising thing about the revival of perfectionistic theories in the 1830s and 1840s is how widespread they were. While one could assume such a revival in Methodism, one would hardly expect to encounter it among Congregationalists and Presbyterians. Yet we find a major movement along this line headed up by Charles Finney, the greatest evangelist of his day. Associated with Finney were Asa Mahan and Charles Fitch (who converted to Millerism in the late 1830s and became one of its foremost leaders).

**Phoebe Palmer: female religious leader
among Methodist perfectionists in the 1840s**

These three men, holding what was known as the Oberlin theology, taught a perfection made possible by the baptism of the Holy Spirit, which empowered and perfected the will of the believer to act in conformity with God's will.

The idea of perfection held during the pre-Civil War years was not merely for personal edification. To the contrary, it had definite social implications. As Ronald Walters puts it, "perfectionism helped create an 'ultraist' mentality which insisted that anything short of millennial standards should not be tolerated, a cast of mind common among antebellum crusaders. It was manifested in such things as utopian efforts to construct a new social order, calls for slavery to end immediately, a belief that any alcohol was evil, and an unwillingness . . . to compromise." The perfectionists of the early nineteenth century didn't want just to be right—they wanted to make things right.

Of course, not all of the perfectionistic theories of the day were healthy. Some believers eventually arrived at the concept that because they were perfect, whatever they did was sinless, since every action of those who were already perfect could not be sin by definition. That belief led some (including some Millerites after the Great Disappointment) into gross transgressions of God's law. Ellen White had to deal with such perversions in her early ministry.

Before moving away from the drive for perfection, we should note that among some individuals it took the form of creating utopian communities where peace and justice would reign. Among the religious there appeared such experiments as the perfectionistic community founded by John Humphrey Noyes at Oneida, New York. More secularized versions of hopeful utopias were Brook Farm and Bronson Alcott's Fruitlands in Massachusetts.

PROTECTING THE "SABBATH"

"Sabbatarianism," penned Robert Abzug, "was clearly the most restorationist of the reform movements of the late 1820s." America's most influential religious leaders had become concerned with lax Sabbath (Sunday) observance in an increasingly pluralistic nation. Lyman Beecher argued that if a "stream of pleasure and of worldly cares" distracted the majority of citizens from Sabbath devotion "irreligion [would] prevail, and immorality and dissoluteness, to an extent utterly inconsistent with the permanence of republican institutions."

Thus Beecher equated Sabbathbreaking with the downfall of the American republic. That idea was not new. The Puritans had brought strict Sunday/Sabbath observance with them from England in the 1630s. Furthermore, seeing themselves as spiritual Israel, the Puritans tied faithfulness in keeping their Sabbath to God's blessing of the faithful and to His cursing of the disobedient, as found in Deuteronomy 27-29. Wanting to be faithful and thus blessed, the Puritan colonies and each of the other colonies passed Sunday laws. Such laws became known as "blue laws" when in 1656 New Haven, Connecticut, enacted a set of Sunday laws printed in England on blue paper.

During the early nineteenth century, religious leaders feared that the nation was breaking the covenant when the law establishing the U.S. Post Office required local postmasters to deliver mail on any day of the week that a person might demand it. By the mid-1820s a rising commercialism in certain urban centers that found it profitable to do business seven days a week joined the problem of Sunday mail.

The upshot was a Sabbatarian campaign based on the same evangelical militancy as drove the other reforms of the era. May

1828 saw the creation of the General Union for Promoting the Observance of the Christian Sabbath. The reform association had as its goal the renewal of Sabbath (Sunday) observance as the key to reviving the specifically Christian structure of social life.

The late 1820s saw a major battle led by Beecher for a law to close down post offices on Sunday and a struggle led by Lewis Tappan and Josiah Bissell to put an end to Sunday business and transport.

The campaign failed, but it set the stage for struggles over Sunday that others would wage much more successfully in the 1880s and 1890s. Ellen White and her Adventist contemporaries would have much to say about that latter conflict.

Meanwhile the early 1840s saw a Sabbath revival of a different type. It would be stimulated by the Seventh Day Baptists, who in 1843 voted, in an uncharacteristically aggressive manner for them, that it was their "solemn duty" to enlighten their fellow citizens on the topic. They also took steps to put that resolution into practice. At their 1844 general conference session they thanked God that "a deeper and wider-spread interest upon the subject has sprung up than has ever before been known in our country."

The most fruitful part of that interest developed among certain areas of Millerite Adventism. It would eventually flow into that sector of post-Disappointment Adventism that would become the Seventh-day Adventist Church. Their belief in the seventh-day Sabbath would put Ellen White and other Seventh-day Adventists in direct confrontation with the revived and powerful Sunday law movement of the 1880s and 1890s (see chapter 8).

THE RISE OF MORMONISM

The same confidence in the "common man" and the same restorationist drive that inspired the rise of so many denominations in the nineteenth century also led to the development of Mormonism. Like so many of his day, young Joseph Smith, of Palmyra, New York, had become discouraged with the established churches. None of them seemingly lined up with God's ideal.

God, Smith said, was reestablishing the true religion through

Joseph Smith, the Mormon Prophet

R&H PUBLISHING ASSOCIATION

him. He claimed to have had an encounter with God the Father and Jesus Christ, who commissioned him to restore the "true church" and the "lost priesthood" to earth. Smith also claimed that the angel Moroni showed him an ancient book written on tablets of gold, which he translated by using magical stones. His so-called translation appeared in 1830 as the *Book of Mormon.* Then on April 6, 1830, he founded his new church. His followers soon became known as Mormons.

Smith, who claimed to be a prophet, espoused the doctrine of polygamy as early as 1836. Before his death in 1844 at the hands of a mob at the Carthage, Illinois, jail, he had married some 49 women, at least 12 of whom already had husbands. By that time Smith had also run for president of the United States, established a private army, and built the well-planned city of Nauvoo, Illinois. Part of his followers moved to found Salt Lake City in the wilderness of Utah in 1847 under the guidance of Brigham Young.

At the heart of Mormon theology is the doctrine of eternal progression. This belief is summarized by the phrase "As man is, God once was; as God is, man may become." Thus human destiny is to evolve into Godhood through obedience to the laws and ordinances of the Utah church.

Unlike the Protestant churches that base their teachings

solely on the Bible, Mormonism holds that such of Smith's writings as the *Book of Mormon,* the *Pearl of Great Price,* and the *Doctrine and Covenants* are canonical. That belief has had a major impact on Mormon doctrinal development. Modern Mormon scholar Stephen E. Robinson tells us that the visions and revelations of Joseph Smith "form the foundation of LDS doctrine. . . . For Latter-day Saints the highest authority in religious matters is continuing revelation from God given through the living apostles and prophets of his church, beginning with Joseph Smith and continuing to the present leadership." With such a view it is not surprising that Mormon theology has deviated from the biblical perspective.

Ellen White, who also claimed the prophetic gift, felt a need to put some distance between her work and that of Smith and the Mormon concept of prophecy (see 2SG iv; 1SM 32). Hers was an evangelical Christian view of the prophetic gift. For her the 66 books of the Bible were the sum total of Scripture. The biblical canon had closed with the book of Revelation. Holding that the Bible was all people needed for salvation, she saw her prophetic function as one of "bringing {her readers} back to the word {the Bible} that they have neglected to follow" (5T 663). On another occasion she penned that her writings were a "lesser light to lead men and women to the greater light {the Bible}" (CM 125).

The Rise of Modern Spiritualism

A few miles from Palmyra in upstate New York another religious phenomenon emerged in 1848. In that year Maggie and Katie Fox set off a spiritualistic excitement that, as Alice Felt Tyler notes, turned into "almost a mania" for the remarkably "large numbers of men and women who became deeply interested in it."

In February 1848 mysterious rappings sounded on the floor, walls, and furniture of whatever room the children happened to be occupying. One night Katie Fox called out, "Here, Mr. Splitfoot, do as I do!" and the mysterious phenomenon replied with the same number of raps as the child gave. Subsequently Mrs. Fox and her daughters worked out a system of communication by which the spirits answered with raps any question asked them.

The sisters eventually became professional mediums, holding public meetings and charging fees as they presented revelation after revelation from the world of the supernatural. Spiritualist societies formed in many towns and villages, and other mediums sprang up all over the country. Before long, table moving, spirit writing, communications with the "dead," and other phenomena that have since become well known in the world of spiritualism joined the mysterious raps. By 1857, 67 spiritualist periodicals in the United States spread the movement's message.

In 1888 Margaret and Katie Fox, as the result of a family quarrel, recanted and sought to expose their career as one great fraud, claiming that they had from the first produced the rappings by cracking the joints of their big toes. Margaret later went

A. F. TYLER, FREEDOM'S FERMENT

The Fox sisters, founders of modern spiritualism

back and claimed that they were not frauds. Their confession had little effect on the spiritualist movement, which argued that the real fraud was the Fox sisters' recantation and not their career.

Ellen White agreed with the spiritualists, claiming that "the mysterious rapping with which modern spiritualism began was not the result of human trickery or cunning, but was the direct work of evil angels, who thus introduced one of the most successful of soul-destroying delusions" (GC 553). According to her, spiritualism would be one of Satan's main tools of deception before the Second Advent (see GC 551-562).

NATIVISM AND ANTI-CATHOLICISM

Nativism is a form of American nationalism that has arisen periodically throughout the history of the United States. It stands over against those things that seem foreign or un-American and is associated with anti-Catholicism though not identical with it. It is closer to being anti-foreign. But it just so happens that the most feared foreigners in nineteenth-century America also happened to be Roman Catholics.

The original settlers of the 13 colonies that became the United States were preponderantly Protestant and largely from Great Britain and Northern and Western Europe. As such, they shared a common base for their cultural and religious values. As noted earlier, Americans came to see themselves as having a millennial mission to the world. That mission had strong ties to the Protestant nature of the republic.

That vision began to face threats during the 1830s as larger numbers of Catholics immigrated to the United States. Around 1830 a Northern newspaper first made the assertion that the Catholic Church was serving as an agent of European governments in an effort to overthrow American democracy. From that time on, the idea of secret Catholic plots permeated Protestant argument.

An anti-Catholic literature developed in the mid-1830s. One influential contribution consisted of a series of letters printed by Samuel F. B. Morse (inventor of the telegraph) in the New York *Observer* in 1834 entitled "A Foreign Conspiracy Against the

Liberties of the United States." The next year Morse published *The Imminent Dangers to the Free Institutions of the United States Through Foreign Immigration.*

That same year the influential Lyman Beecher released *A Plea for the West.* In that work Beecher compared the immigrant threat to the Mississippi Valley to an invasion of Egyptian locusts or northern barbarians. Beecher left no doubt that if Protestant America was to fulfill its mission to the world the nation would have to save the West from Catholicism.

Along a different line were Rebecca Reed's *Six Months in a Convent* (1835) and Maria Monk's *Awful Disclosures of the Hôtel Dieu Nunnery of Montreal* (1836). Monk's best-seller, set forth as an autobiographical account, told of how she had become a convert to Catholicism and a nun. She then suggestively described

HARPER'S WEEKLY

Every Catholic immigrant was viewed by nativists as an agent sent by the pope to subvert American Protestantism.

the types of sin she experienced behind convent walls as she joined other novices and nuns in a prostitute's life. Even though later events proved Monk to be a fraud, the book still did its damage in an inflammatory age.

Even more ugly than the anti-Catholic publications was occasional mass violence. In 1834, for example, a mob burned down a Catholic convent near Boston. A few other attacks occurred on Catholic schools and churches during the late 1830s and early 1840s. But the most serious violence took place in Philadelphia in 1844, where Irish Catholics fought back against the nativists. The several days of street fighting led to 13 deaths, 50 people wounded, and the arson of two Catholic churches.

The latter part of the 1840s saw the foreign/Catholic threat expand as massive numbers of Irish Catholics fled to the United States in the wake of the terrible potato famine of 1846 and as large numbers of German Catholics left their homeland after the abortive revolution of 1848. Whereas in 1840 the Roman Catholic Church was the fifth-largest denomination in the United States, by 1850 it was the largest. Yet that was merely the beginning. Between 1850 and 1860 the number of foreign-born in the United States nearly doubled. The immigrants came in such numbers that they were able to form their own communities in which they retained their Old World language, culture, and way of life.

The high point of nativism took place in the 1850s when the movement had its own national political party. The American or "Know-Nothing" Party had dozens of state legislators and several congressional representatives elected in 1854, but it soon lost its strength as public interest shifted to the disruptions over slavery that led up to the Civil War. Another wave of anti-Catholicism would arise in the 1880s and 1890s in the face of labor strife and further immigration.

Ellen White did not partake of the violence or the political action aimed at the Catholic Church and its members. Nor did she appear to have any particular fear of foreign domination. On the other hand, through the study of Bible prophecy she did be-

BAILEY, AMERICAN PAGEANT

Nativist cartoon depicting Irish and German immigrants stealing an election.

lieve that the Papacy *as an institution* in conjunction with an apostate Protestantism would play a part in end-time events (GC 579-581). We must counterbalance that belief by her repeated counsel for Adventists not to make "hard thrusts" against the church of Rome, and the fact that many conscientious Christians in the Catholic Church were living up to the light they had better than some Seventh-day Adventists. She tended to see individual Catholics as souls who could have a closer walk with God as they saw the gospel more clearly (9T 243; CW 64, 65; Ev 144, 574).

Chapter Five

Technological Advances

The early nineteenth century was not merely an era of millennial hope and reform enthusiasm and religious innovation; it was also a period of technological advance. In fact, without the technological revolution the reform and religious movements of the day would have experienced less success.

Steam power transformed transportation and mass communications. One has only to think of such innovations as the railroad, steamboats, and the steam-powered printing press to begin to grasp the magnitude of the transformation. Outside of the realm of steam power we find inventions such as the telegraph. In this chapter we will limit ourselves largely to the printing revolution and the railroad, since those two innovations impacted most directly on Ellen White's ministry.

THE PUBLISHING REVOLUTION

Just as the Protestant Reformation of the sixteenth century owes a great deal of its success to the invention of movable type by Gutenberg in 1453, so does the spread of the reform and religious ideologies of the early nineteenth century depend on a comparable printing revolution. Not only did the steam press speed up the process of printing after 1822, but so did the advent of machine papermaking and paper-cutting machines.

The result was phenomenal. In 1833, for example, New York's *Courier and Enquirer,* with 4,500 readers, had the largest readership in the city. It cost six cents a copy. Just two years later the New York *Sun* published a run of 53,000 in one day at a penny a copy. In those two years output went from 200 to 5,500 copies per hour and from 2,000 to 55,000 per day.

The American Antislavery Society immediately picked up the new technology and began to blanket the entire nation with printed material—more than a million pieces in 1835 alone. The success of that campaign would not be lost on a young associate of William Lloyd Garrison's by the name of Joshua V. Himes.

The widespread use of the press by social reformers and religious groups had begun before the advent of the penny newspaper, but the declining cost of printing greatly accelerated the trend. One ecstatic clergyman noted in 1839 that "a well-conducted religious periodical is like a thousand preachers, flying in almost as many directions, by means of horses, mailstages, steam boats, railroad cars, ships, etc., etc., offering life and salvation to the sons of men in almost every clime." In 1823 the *Methodist Magazine* observed that "a religious newspaper would have been a phenomenon not many years since, but now the groaning press throws them out in almost every direction." By 1830 the United States had 605 religious periodicals, of which only 14 had existed before 1790. Also by 1830 the American Bible Society and the American Tract Society were annually producing more than 1 million Bibles and 6 million tracts, respectively.

The Millerites under the leadership of Himes caught the spirit of the new age of print. One author referred to Himes as the "Napoleon of the press." And Nathan Hatch, a leading historian of American religion, has described Himes' publishing efforts as "an unprecedented media blitz" and "an unprecedented communications crusade." In roughly four years during the early 1840s Himes oversaw the distribution of more than 5 million pieces of Millerite literature—nearly one for every four people in the United States.

The Sabbatarian Adventists followed the Millerite example. One of the secrets of their success was the aggressive spread of their message through publications. Ellen White and her husband marched at the very forefront of that drive. Not only did she tell the church that Adventist publications "are to be scattered abroad like the leaves of autumn" (4T 79), but she suggested that "in a large degree through our publishing houses is to be accomplished" the final work of the church on earth (7T 140).

One result of such counsel is that as of the late 1990s Seventh-day Adventists operated 55 publishing houses around the world printing material in more than 235 languages. Ellen White herself, with her writings having been translated into nearly 150 languages, is the most widely translated female author in history and the most widely translated American author of either sex.

PROGRESS IN TRANSPORTATION

If the publishing revolution allowed the printed word to go everywhere, advances in transportation also permitted the living preacher to be many more places than was previously possible. One of the improvements that aided Ellen White in her work was steam applied to watercraft. Thus steam-powered ships helped speed her crossings of the Atlantic and Pacific, while steamboats carried her along rivers and canals in the United States.

But it wasn't steam applied to boats that made the most difference in enriching her ministry. Rather it was the railroad. A rather primitive contraption in her early years, by the late 1860s the railroad spanned the United States and enabled Ellen White and others to traverse the nation in relative rapidity as they sought to make camp meeting appointments and other assignments. The railroad allowed one to go places in days that a few years previously took months. The absence of the railroad would have greatly curtailed Ellen White's ministry. Travel on the "cars" made it possible for her and others to have truly national ministries.

But rail travel wasn't all that easy, even if it was an improvement over previous means. It required a great deal of stamina in

HARPER'S WEEKLY

Travel by rail was far from comfortable.

Rail travel was also far from safe.

the Civil War years and in the decades that followed. Ventilation was generally poor and the heating in winter notoriously uneven. Scheduling was often erratic, with meal stops atrocious unless one brought a lunch basket. In the summer open windows brought in a multitude of coal cinders while closed windows made the air hot, heavy, and polluted with the odor of whiskey, tobacco, and closely packed bodies. The wooden seats were uncomfortable. Rail travel was anything but pleasant. As Lucius Beebe (a friend of the railroads) put it, "the American public rode to dusty destinies in regimented discomfort."

Besides their discomfort, the trains could also be quite deadly. While undoubtedly safer than horse travel, which had 10 times the fatality rate of the modern automobile, as late as 1890 railroads still caused some 10,000 deaths and 80,000 serious injuries per year in the United States alone. That works out to nearly 30 deaths and 230 serious injuries *per day*. Compared with standards in the 1890s, travel by modern railroads and airplanes is infinitely safer. Part of the problem was that the pursuit of profits ignored the safety of passengers and rail workers. George T. Strong responded to the safety issue by writing that "we shall never travel safely till some pious, wealthy, and much beloved railroad director has been hanged for murder."

James and Ellen White had their own brush with railroad tragedy in 1854 in an accident that killed at least four and seriously injured many more (see 1Bio 294-297). Even though Ellen White frequently remarked about the problems associated with rail travel, she was also quite convinced that the railroad was an overall blessing in spreading the three angels' messages. "By means of railroads and steamboat lines," she wrote, "we are connected with every part of the world and given access to every nation with our message of truth" (5T 381). As she saw it, the transportation advances of the nineteenth century had allowed Seventh-day Adventism to become a truly worldwide movement by the year 1900.

Ellen White's World After the Civil War

Symbols of the new age: the railroad and Charles Darwin

Chapter Six

A Changing World

The great turning point in American history was the nation's Civil War (1861-1865). The transformations that took place during the era of the war and its aftermath eventually infiltrated every realm of American existence. This chapter will examine changes in the social and intellectual realms.

SOCIAL CHANGES

Foremost among the social changes was industrialization. Prior to the 1860s the Jeffersonian ideal of a great rural republic, with the majority of the people living on and working their own land, had prevailed. Jefferson dreamed of a nation free from the degradation of great cities and the slavery of factories and coal pits that he had seen in England. Through such agencies as the Louisiana Purchase Jefferson believed that the republic had enough land "for the thousandth and thousandth generation."

Neither Jefferson nor his contemporaries foresaw how rapidly their visions of an agrarian nation would crumble. Even before the war (in 1860) the capital invested in industry, railroads, commerce, and urban property exceeded the value of farms. But the coming of the war literally escalated industrial growth into an industrial explosion that began with the need to supply a vast army but did not end with the cessation of hostilities.

The railroad stood at the center of the new industrial expansion. Rail networks opened fresh markets for manufactured goods and sped the country's abundant raw materials to the factory. Combined with the railroads in transforming the economic base of the nation were newly invented laborsaving machinery, new ways of financing massive business endeavors through monopolistic trusts, a supply of cheap labor made possible through immigration, and an ever-expanding market fed by the same never-ending tide of immigrants.

The United States was the world's foremost industrial nation by 1894. But the industrial transformation had widened the rift between the nation's rich and poor. By 1900 about one tenth of the population owned and controlled nine tenths of the country's wealth and a new class had arisen—the millionaire.

Jefferson's agrarian dream was in the process of turning into an industrial nightmare as business tycoons sought every advantage in a competitive marketplace fueled by the Darwinian philosophy of the survival of the fittest. Thomas Bailey has pointed out that John D. Rockefeller "wielded more influence over more people than many kings."

Meanwhile, the working person "was becoming a lever puller in a giant mechanism." Whereas before the Civil War laborers may have toiled in a small plant in which the owner greeted them in the morning by their first names, now factory employees worked for a depersonalized and generally conscienceless corporation whose highest goal was to maximize profits—all too often at the expense of workers. Thus the stage had been set for conflict between labor and capital.

A second social transformation in the post-Civil War period was the changing size and nature of immigration. The 90 years running from 1820 through 1910 witnessed one of the largest mass migrations in human history. The following graph helps us get somewhat of a grasp of the sheer numbers involved.

Immigration to the United States between 1865 and 1910 was not only high in sheer numbers, but also reflected what most

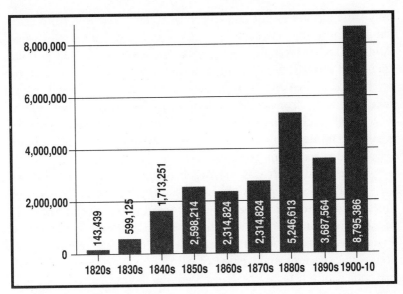

Immigration by decades

Americans perceived to be a qualitative shift. Before the 1880s the bulk of immigrants had a relatively easy time assimilating. Most of them came from the British Isles and Western and Northern Europe and were usually Protestants, except for the Irish and German Catholics that were discussed in chapter 4. Such peoples enjoyed a comparatively high degree of literacy and were accustomed to some form of constitutional government.

But the "new immigration" of the decades following 1880 represented a different type. For the first time a substantial proportion of the new arrivals came from Southern and Eastern Europe. The new immigration was non-Teutonic, predominantly Roman Catholic, generally illiterate and poverty-stricken, and had often left nations ruled by despotic governments. Beyond that, they tended to live together in "Little Italys" and "Little Polands" in such cities as New York and Chicago, where they maintained their native languages, religions, and customs.

By the first decade of the twentieth century the new immigration constituted 66 percent of the total flow. The newcomers not only were numerous but had a high birth rate. Old-line Americans feared that a sea of strange people would inundate the original Anglo-Saxon Protestant stock and would soon be able to outvote them and thus derail the United States from its millennial mission to the world. The fact that the newer immigrants were willing to take jobs away from old-line Americans by working for "starvation" wages didn't endear them to the established working classes, while the moneyed classes feared their importation of such foreign ideologies as socialism, communism, and anarchism.

The natural result was a resurgence of nativism (see chapter 4). Notorious among nativist groups was the American Protective Association, created in 1887. Such organizations were not only anti-immigrant but more specifically anti-Catholic. The American Protective Association, for example, pledged its members "to strike the shackles and chains of blind obedience to the Roman Catholic Church from the hampered and bound consciences of a priest-ridden and church-oppressed people."

Closely related to the new immigration and industrialization in the post-Civil War world was urbanization. In a relatively short period of time the United States went from a nation of farms and villages to one of increasingly large urban areas. In 1860 no American city could boast 1 million inhabitants, but by 1890 New York, Chicago, and Philadelphia had moved beyond the million mark. In 1900 New York, with some 3.5 million residents, was the second-largest city in the world. The growth of medium-sized cities kept apace with the giants. Thus the number of towns with populations of 100,000 or more leaped from 9 in 1860 to 38 in 1900 to 68 in 1920.

The pull of the city varied for different people. For some it centered on higher-paying jobs in the rising factory system that dotted the urban landscape. For others the bright lights, anonymity, and freedom to "have fun" contrasted favorably with the boredom of the farm and the tight surveillance of the small town. And for the increasing number of poorer immigrants from Southern and Eastern Europe the ethnic city ghetto drew them because they had nowhere else to go.

While the cities held advantages for certain people, they also had their problems. Not the least had to do with vice, overcrowding, and sanitation (see chapter 9).

One of the great challenges of the Progressive social reformers who arose around the turn of the century was how to clean up the cities in terms of crime, vice, and just plain filth. Others claimed that the answer to the problems of the city was to turn their backs to it. Thus the Country Life Movement enjoyed a brief vogue in the early years of the twentieth century. Another challenge of the cities was how to evangelize the urban masses, many of whom were either Catholics or had lost contact with their Protestantism when they moved to the "big city."

Ellen White had concerns about the city that paralleled those of the larger culture. She definitely expressed the Jeffersonian concerns of the Country Life Movement with its anti-city view of the good life. But beyond that ideal, between 1890 and 1910 she encouraged the Adventist leadership ever more stridently to put forth "untiring effort in behalf of the millions living within the shadow of impending doom" in the large cities, where the "wickedness of the wicked is almost beyond comprehension" (Ev 25).

The city and its challenges was not the only aspect of the transformed social world that she would address. Chapter 9, for example, will briefly indicate her reaction to the issues raised in the struggle between capital and labor.

INTELLECTUAL CHANGES

The transformation of the intellectual world of the post-Civil War years was just as radical as changes in the social world. Foremost among those shifts would be the rise of Darwinism, the comparative religious movement, and biblical criticism.

Modern evolution looks back to 1859, the year that Charles Darwin published *The Origin of Species,* for its beginning point. In essence Darwin set forth the theory that all living things developed from simple forms through a process of evolution and natural selection. His view was a shift from the traditional Christian position, which held that the creation of the world occurred exactly as described in the book of Genesis.

In the 1830s Charles Lyell had moved away from the traditional position in his *Principles of Geology.* As a result, some theologians had begun to talk of the six days of Creation as being thousands of years each. But Darwin's thesis of natural selection and survival of the fittest took the battle from the remoter world of geology into the nearer realm of biology.

Darwin threw gasoline on an already hot fire in 1871 with the publication of *The Descent of Man,* which traced the evolutionary origin and development of humanity rather than the general forms of life. *Descent* not only questioned the veracity of the Bible's Creation narrative but also undermined traditional conceptions of sin, morality, and human dignity.

Needless to say, Darwin's theory split the Christian community. Many Protestants concluded that if Darwin was correct, then the Bible must be wrong. Thus we find Princeton's Charles Hodge proclaiming in 1874 that Darwinism in the final analysis "is atheism." On the other hand, Harvard's John Fiske claimed that "evolution is God's way of doing things." Fiske and many others in the liberal wing of Protestantism held that God would use endless evolutionary improvement in human nature to bring about peace on earth and eventually usher in the millennial kingdom of God.

The theory of evolution brought about an intellectual revolution in the Western world that would eventually infiltrate nearly every area of scholarly endeavor. In the process, the dominant role of the Bible in shaping the frameworks of human understanding would give way to science as the primary authority. Within the Protestant community between the 1870s and the 1920s the theory of evolution would become increasingly more divisive, until it became one of the issues that split Protestantism into conservative and liberal wings (see chapter 8).

And what did Ellen White think about the issue? She stood firmly in the camp of the creationists. "There is," she wrote, "no ground for the supposition that man was evolved by slow degrees of development from the lower forms of animal or vegetable life. Such teaching lowers the great work of the Creator to the level of man's narrow, earthly conceptions" (PP 45). She held not only for a six-day creation, but also to the Bible as the authority that provides a framework for understanding science. Also she held that science "brings from her research nothing that, rightly understood, conflicts with divine revelation" (Ed 128).

It didn't take long for the central ideas of biological evolution to jump the fence into the social realm. Herbert Spencer became the leading thinker of what came to be known as social Darwinism. Spencer applied such ideas as survival of the fittest to the development of society and social institutions in a pattern that moved from primitive social institutions to complex. His ideas spread rapidly, and, as Richard Hofstadter has noted, "in the three decades after the Civil War it was impossible to be active in any field of intellectual work without mastering Spencer."

Social Darwinism became a dominant ideal in an age of a rampant capitalism that held for free and unregulated competition. The law of the jungle and survival of the fittest in the economic realm set the stage for much thinking about the social order in the new industrial world of the late nineteenth century.

William Graham Sumner, America's foremost social Darwinist, noted that such a theory "bears harshly on the weak." But, he pointed out, "if we do not like the survival of the fittest, we have only one possible alternative, and that is the survival of the unfittest. . . . A plan for nourishing the unfittest and yet advancing in civilization, no man will ever find." Sumner also held that "millionaires are a product of natural selection."

And what are the real-life implications of such a theory? That the strong should get stronger and richer while the weak should be left to dwindle on the evolutionary vine. Thus public welfare and even public education are contrary to the advance of civilization.

Such sentiments even found their way into the pulpit—especially those pulpits that pandered to wealthy congregations. Phillips Brooks preached that "no man in this land suffers from poverty unless it be more than his fault—unless it be his sin."

And in 1877 the finely dressed Henry Ward Beecher could casti-gate striking railway workers who had lost 30 percent of their salary in three years for not being content with their current wages of a dollar a day. "It is said," he pontificated, "that a dollar a day is not enough for a wife and five or six children. . . . Is not a dollar a day enough to buy bread with? Water costs nothing; and a man who cannot live on bread is not fit to live. What is the use of a civilization that simply makes men incompetent to live under the conditions which exist?"

Another clerical representative of social Darwinian economics was Russell H. Conwell, who preached his "Acres of Diamonds" sermon to more than 6,000 audiences with total earnings from honorariums and royalties of some $8 million. According to Conwell, it is our God-given "duty to get rich." Furthermore, poverty results from an individual's sins. Thus "to sympathize with a man whom God has punished for his sins, thus to help him when God would still continue a just punishment, is to do wrong."

Ellen White had a different outlook on poverty and aiding the poor. While she realized that some poverty did come from one's own fault, she also recognized that "there are multitudes struggling with poverty, compelled to labor hard for small wages, unable to secure the barest necessities of life." Along with the apostle James and the Old Testament prophets she opposed those "rich men" and business practices that oppressed the poor (9T 90, 91). She had a genuine concern for them. In the spirit of Christ, welfare ministry for the underprivileged was close to her heart and practice.

The theory of evolution not only shaped thought in the bio-logical, social, and economic realms but also dominated certain sectors of religious thought. That was especially true in the com-parative religions movement. Such theologians as James Freeman Clarke pictured the evolution of religion from the primitive to the complex, with Christianity being the most evolved of the world's great religions. Thus Christianity was not unique. It was merely the leading edge of what all religions were evolving into. Ethics rather than the cross stood at the center of Clarke's version of religion. He held that "universal unity is the object and end of Christianity" as the various world religions evolved toward the kingdom of God, with Christianity leading the way.

Beyond the various Darwinian trends in religious thought, the United States in the latter part of the nineteenth century also witnessed the rise of the scientific or critical study of the Bible. Having its roots in Germany, the movement made its way to America soon after the Civil War through scholars who studied abroad, accepted the ideas of their German teachers, and began to present them in American seminaries and universities.

The proponents of the higher critical method applied modern philosophical presuppositions to the Bible. They discarded traditional theories of inspiration and began to view the Bible as a human production without supernatural guidance in its writing. Thus scholars came to think of the Bible as a compilation of poetry, history, folklore, and prophecy that human beings had assembled over a period of a thousand years or so. As such, scholars treated the Bible as if it were merely another book that should be studied like any other book through the methods of textual analysis.

Not only did the biblical critics discard the miraculous elements of the Bible, but they doubted the trustworthiness of the information it contained. Thus they claimed, for example, that the stories of Genesis displayed the same sort of superstitious mythology as other ancient documents and that prophecy was not predictive but had been written after the events it described. Additionally, the critics read the Bible through the eyes of the evolutionary hypothesis. In the process the Bible lost its authority as not only being a reliable history but also as an authoritative source for doctrinal formation.

By the end of the nineteenth century the widespread acceptance of the evolutionary hypothesis and the presuppositions undergirding the critical study of the Bible had swept aside the underpinnings of traditional Christian understandings. It had laid the groundwork for the development of Protestant liberalism, a topic we will return to in chapter 8.

We have seen in this chapter that momentous changes took

place in both the social and intellectual worlds of the late nineteenth and early twentieth centuries. Such transformations provided the larger context in which Ellen White lived and ministered. They and other shifts that we will discuss in subsequent chapters set the stage for many of the issues that Ellen White would have to deal with in the second half of her life.

Chapter Seven

Millennial Visions

We noted in chapter 1 that millennial themes had pre-occupied the United States before the Civil War. That interest did not disappear after the war, but it did take on some new flavors.

PREMILLENNIAL PERSPECTIVES

In spite of its "Great Disappointment" when Christ did not come in 1844, Millerite Adventism lived on. But after that date it was no longer a unified movement. Rather, Millerism split into several denominations, with the Seventh-day Adventist branch of the movement starting out as the weakest but ending up by far the strongest by the time of Ellen White's death in 1915.

By that time the once-powerful Evangelical Adventist denomination had all but ceased to exist, while the Advent Christian movement had stagnated evangelistically. On the other hand, the Seventh-day Adventists had entered into an ever-accelerating program of worldwide missions as its membership continued to multiply. I argued in *Millennial Fever and the End of the World* that the reason for the success of Seventh-day Adventism was that it had remained faithful to Miller's prophetic insights and had come to see itself as a people of prophecy with a commission rooted in Revelation 14:6-12 to preach the message of the three angels to all the earth. By way of contrast, the other ex-Millerite groups had given up Miller's understanding of Bible prophecy and had largely lost their reason for existing as separate religious bodies. In short, the secret of Seventh-day Adventism's success has been its sense of prophetic identity. Ellen White was a foremost influence in helping Adventism understand that identity and the missiological responsibilities it entailed.

In spite of its relative success in the latter part of the nineteenth century, Seventh-day Adventism was not the largest or most influential premillennial group in the United States after the Civil War. That distinction belongs to the dispensationalist movement, which began its rapid interdenominational growth in the 1870s and 1880s. Conservative American Christians in the post-Civil War years were quite open to premillennialism. To many it appeared that the world was becoming worse rather than better. As a result, they tended to reject postmillennialism with its teaching that conditions would get better and better until the kingdom of God was established on earth, and to accept premillennial theologies that held that the solution to the world's problems was the second advent of Jesus at the beginning of the millennium.

But where could they turn? After all, most Protestants held that 1844 had "discredited" Millerite forms of prophetic understanding. A premillennial theology developed earlier in the century in Great Britain by John Nelson Darby now filled the void. Whereas the Millerites and Seventh-day Adventists held to the historicist school of prophetic interpretation, the dispensationalists were futurists. Historicism views apocalyptic prophecy as unfolding continuously from the time of the biblical prophets to the second coming of Jesus, while futurism sees most apocalyptic prophecy having its fulfillment immediately before the Second Advent. From the dispensationalist perspective, no fulfillments of prophecy have taken place since the death of the apostles, even though such events as the return of the Jews to Israel are preparing the way for the final fulfillments.

Key elements in the dispensational scheme of understanding

R&H PUBLISHING ASSOCIATION

1878 prophetic conference in New York City. Premillennialism was far from dead, but it was moving toward dispensationalism.

include the central role of Israel in end-time events, the secret rapture, and the idea that God has had several different dispensations, or periods (usually seven), throughout the history of the world. During each dispensation God approaches the problem of sin and salvation in a different manner. Thus, for example, God's dealings with sinners varied between the dispensation of grace and the dispensation of law.

Darby's dispensationalism came to the United States in the 1870s when he toured the country and won a number of influential evangelical pastors to his cause. It spread rapidly in conservative circles through the medium of prophetic conferences. By the late 1870s we even find such ex-Millerite leaders as Josiah Litch (the third most influential man in Millerism) and Henry Dana Ward (chair of the first Millerite general conference) moving toward the dispensationalist camp.

In spite of its problematic interpretations of salvation and prophecy, dispensationalism found an easy alliance with other conservative evangelicals. Timothy Weber, a foremost historian of the movement, suggests that the development of Darwinism and higher criticism encouraged the alliance. "The rise of theological liberalism," Weber notes, "forced all conservative evangelicals into a close, defensive alliance" and "dispensationalists received a hearty welcome" that would not have been forthcoming in less stressful times. In 1909 dispensationalism received a major boost through the publication of the *Scofield Reference Bible.*

POSTMILLENNIAL PERSPECTIVES

Whereas large numbers of conservative Protestants turned to premillennialism in the years after the Civil War, many liberal Protestants continued in their postmillennial belief. In fact, their postmillennialism integrated quite nicely with their recently accepted Darwinian philosophy. For many liberals evolution was not merely God's way of doing things, it was God's way of bringing about the kingdom of God on earth.

Thus John Fiske could argue that the final end of "the working of natural selection upon man" would be the throwing off of his "brute inheritance" and the achievement of peace on earth. Fiske unabashedly claimed that "it is Darwinism which has placed Humanity upon a higher pinnacle than ever. The future is lighted for us with the radiant colours of hope. Strife and sorrow shall disappear. Peace and love shall reign supreme. . . . We may look forward to the time when in the truest sense the kingdoms of this world shall become the kingdom of Christ, and he shall reign for ever and ever, king of kings and lord of lords."

Along a similar line of reasoning, James Freeman Clarke in his explicitly evolutionary treatment of the world's great religions concludes that "the millennium has not arrived. . . . The sword is not yet beaten into a ploughshare, nor has universal peace arrived. Yet such is the *inevitable tendency* of things. As knowledge spreads, as wealth increases, as the moral force of the world is enlarged, law, more and more, takes the place of force. Men no longer wear swords. . . . Towns are no longer fortified with walls. . . . They are all folded in the peaceful arms of natural law. *So far the atonement has prevailed.* Only nations still continue to fight; but the time is at hand when international law, the parliament of the world, the confederation of man, shall take the place of standing armies and iron-clad navies" (italics supplied).

Time and social reform were the key elements in liberal eschatology. As humans improved and made social iniquities right the kingdoms of earth would evolve into the kingdom of God. Thus we find an emphasis in the liberal wing of Protestantism on the social gospel and social reform (see chapter 8). At the root of the liberal understanding was the idea that human beings were becoming better and better and would continue to do so through education and other forms of social improvement fueled by the ceaseless process of evolution.

NATIONAL MILLENNIAL PERSPECTIVES

Standing alongside of and often intertwined with distinctly religious millennial perspectives was an ongoing vision of the millennial destiny of the United States. Senator Albert J. Beveridge, speaking to the Senate near the turn of the century on the topic of American imperialistic responsibility, helps us see the shape of that vision. "God," he claimed, "has not been preparing the English-speaking Teutonic peoples for a thousand years for nothing but vain and idle self-contemplation and self-admiration. No. He made us master organizers of the world to establish system where chaos reigned. . . . He has made us adept in government that we may administer government among savage and senile peoples. Were it not for such a force as this the world would relapse into barbarism and night. And of all our race He has marked the American people as His chosen nation to finally lead in the redemption of the world."

Clergyman Josiah Strong sounded a similar trumpet blast in his influential *Our Country* in 1885. "Our plea," Strong penned, "is not America for America's sake; but America for the world's sake. For, if this generation is faithful to its trust, America is to become God's right arm in his battle with the world's ignorance and oppression and sin. . . . Ours is the elect nation for the age to come. We are the chosen people. We cannot afford to wait. The plans of God will not wait. Those plans seem to have brought us to one of the closing stages in the world's career, in which we can no longer *drift* with safety to our destiny." " 'America Christianized means the *world* Christianized.' And 'If America fails,' says Professor Park, 'the *world* will fail.' During this crisis, Christian work {to keep the nation Protestant and faithful to God} is unspeakably more important in the United States than anywhere else in the world."

Such strains of national millennialism inspired President Woodrow Wilson to lead the United States into World War I as a crusade to end all wars and to make the world safe for democracy. In a similar vein, it was a national millennial vision coupled with a faithfulness to God implied in God's covenant with America that inspired continuing pressure to maintain the United States as a Christian nation that upheld all of God's laws, including those laws connected with Sunday sacredness.

Chapter Eight

Religious Impulses

The changing world of the late nineteenth century had a definite effect upon the religious developments of the day. Varying responses to new intellectual developments would progressively drive a wedge into the midst of evangelical Protestantism that eventually would split the movement into fundamentalist and modernist wings. Beyond that, religion would employ the organizational strategies and methodologies of big business to evangelize the new urban metropolises. In addition, the greatest emphasis in foreign missions in the history of Protestantism would accompany the last great surge of foreign imperialism by the United States and the Western European powers in the 1890s. Religious developments in the last half of the nineteenth century would literally change the face of the religious landscape.

REVIVALISM AND THE ROLE OF D. L. MOODY

One of the most visible features of late-nineteenth-century religion was the conspicuous success of Dwight L. Moody. Born to a family of modest means, Moody early set his heart on becoming a successful capitalist. And he might have developed into one of the Carnegies, Rockefellers, or McCormicks of the day except for his profound conversion to Christianity in the 1850s.

Thereafter he devoted his considerable entrepreneurial talents to the business of winning souls.

Whereas Charles Finney in the 1820s and 1830s had achieved his greatest success in communities in which the population rarely exceeded 10,000, the focal points of Moody's efforts were the great cities of a million or more. Such cities contained multitudes who had departed farms and small towns for the excitement and possibilities of the city. In the process many had left behind their religious affiliations and practices, which was quite easy to do in a world in which the social pressures of the rural community no longer weighed upon them. Besides that large group of indigenous unchurched were the hundreds of thousands of new immigrants with their strange customs and non-Protestant religions.

As a New England country boy, Moody knew that "water runs downhill," and he was convinced that in the life of the nation "the highest hills are the cities." If the cities could be won for Protestantism, Moody held, "we shall stir the whole nation." The conservative moneyed classes in general shared Moody's hopes. Fearing the danger of an unconverted proletariat, they gave their money and moral support to Moody's revival crusades even though they seemed to be interested more in social stability than in his evangelical message itself.

His meetings brought the zeal of the camp meeting to the big city. Combined with that enthusiasm were the organizational skills developed by industry and business. A Moody crusade left nothing to chance. Committees existed for everything, even an executive committee to make sure that the other committees functioned properly. Moody also used modern advertising to utmost advantage. When one person complained that it was undignified to advertise religious services, Moody shot back that he thought it more dignified than to preach to empty pews.

Moody's pews were anything but empty. His evangelistic teams organized along the lines of mass industry to process the raw material of the populous cities into a finished Protestant product.

MOODY BIBLE INSTITUTE

Moody preaching to thousands in London.

His techniques would set the pattern for the mass evangelism of Billy Sunday and Billy Graham in the twentieth century.

Moody's theological message was simple. The three R's of the gospel were that people had been ruined by sin, redeemed by Christ, and could be regenerated by the Holy Ghost. All they had to do in order to be saved was to will to believe. Moody preached with a sense of urgency. "I look upon this world as a wrecked vessel," he claimed. "God has given me a lifeboat and said to me, 'Moody, save all you can.'" He didn't care so much what denomination individuals chose to join, just so long as they got in a lifeboat.

Two aspects of Moody's theology had an especially large impact on the changing Protestantism of the late nineteenth and early twentieth centuries. The first was that he was a premillennialist and emphasized the second coming of Christ as the only solution for a world hopelessly lost in sin. That emphasis did much to prepare many conservatives to accept the developing dispensationalism of the day (see chapter 7).

A second aspect of Moody's theology that influenced the Protestant world of his day was its lack of content. That lack, coupled with the fact that Moody insisted that all the major

Protestant churches unite in supporting his citywide crusades, undoubtedly made for an *outward* union of liberals and conservatives. But that external coalition may have had the long-term effect of heightening the crisis in Protestantism in the early twentieth century, since the real differences between the modernists and fundamentalists had been growing out of sight until it was too late for moderate discussion of the type that would have earlier come to the fore had there not been the tranquilizing effect of a popular *apparent* unity.

THE RISE OF PROTESTANT LIBERALISM

One of the central religious issues of the late nineteenth century was how to relate to the new intellectual and social developments then inundating the Western world (see chapter 6). One response came to be known as Protestant liberalism or modernism.

In actuality the liberal response was a sincere attempt to preserve the Christian faith by adjusting traditional Christianity to issues in modern culture. Unfortunately, the process led to such a transformation of beliefs that Protestant liberalism hardly resembled the faith handed down from the Reformers.

While liberal Protestantism had had some presence in the United States before the Civil War through such movements as Unitarianism and Transcendentalism, it wasn't until after the war that liberalism found a growing place in the mainline Protestant denominations. And even though the various liberal theologians differed from each other, they tended to hold to certain prominent principles and themes.

Central to the liberal belief system was the immanence of God in nature and history. Modernists argued that God was present in and revealed through the progress of history and culture. God worked through natural law in general and through the process of evolution in particular. The liberals with their high view of science virtually cast out all miracles, including such central Christian beliefs as the incarnation and resurrection of Jesus.

A second pillar in the liberal scheme of things was that human beings were essentially good. Thus they had a highly optimistic view of humanity's potential to improve itself as individuals worked for the common good. Being on the cutting edge of evolution, human beings could be God's agents to help bring about the kingdom of God on earth.

A third liberal belief held that sin is not rebellion against God but a matter of ignorance and/or the bestial remains of an evolutionary inheritance. Such a belief implied that what we needed to clean up the sin problem was not conversion but education and social reform. Educated people would naturally do what was right.

A fourth liberal concept had to do with Jesus. They discounted the substitutionary sacrifice and upheld Jesus as the best example of what an individual could become.

Closely tied to their "example" rather than "Saviour" understanding of Jesus was the liberal substitution of ethics (correct conduct) for doctrine (correct belief) at the center of their understanding of Christianity. Doctrine and creeds were relics of the past.

A sixth pillar of liberalism involved an evolutionary understanding of Scripture itself. The Bible was no longer a supernatural production of the Holy Spirit, but a collection of myths and primitive understandings much like those found in other underdeveloped cultures. Thus the Bible was not so much God's revelation to humanity as humanity's grasping after God. Such a belief allowed liberals to embrace the radical results of higher criticism and evolutionary science without qualms.

A seventh centerpiece of liberalism stated that the mission of the church was to help bring in the kingdom of God through religious education and social reform. That belief led them to highlight what became known as the Social Gospel as the church became active in righting the social wrongs created by rapid urbanization and industrialization in the late nineteenth century. To the Social Gospelers Christianity needed to apply the ethics of Jesus not just to individual lives but to economic and political structures as well. As in pre-Civil War postmillennialism, the kingdom of God could not come until social reform had done its job.

The beginning of the twentieth century found the liberals in a state of confidence in the future progress of the kingdom of God. One of their leaders in 1900 wrote that "we are going into a century more full of hope, and promise, and opportunity than any period in the world's history." Such a faith had no inkling of the two world wars, the Great Depression, and the atomic threat that would do so much to obliterate the liberal vision.

THE CONSERVATIVE REACTION

To put it mildly, not all Protestants were enamored with what many came to call the New Theology. Nor did liberalism gain control of the mainline denominations easily or quickly. The process would extend from the 1870s up through the late 1920s, with the liberal faction ever making larger inroads in the Northern branches of such churches as the Presbyterians, Methodists, and Baptists. But large and powerful conservative factions remained in every denomination.

Conservative evangelicals tended to view the liberal accommodation to science and culture as a sellout of basic Christianity. Across the post-Civil War decades they would grow aggressively more militant as they sought to protect and define what they saw as the essence of Christianity. Their definitions, of course, reacted to the liberal agenda.

In 1910 the Northern Presbyterian General assembly adopted a five-point declaration of "essential" doctrines. They included (1) the inerrancy of Scripture, (2) the virgin birth of Christ, (3) His substitutionary atonement, (4) His bodily resurrection, and (5) the authenticity of miracles. It was not the first such list, nor would it be the last. Some groups with a dispensationalist orientation substituted the premillennial return of Christ for point 5 in the Presbyterian list. Others emphasized the importance of creation over evolution, the degradedness of human nature and the necessity of salvation through faith in Christ's sacrifice, and the verbal nature of inspiration. In fact, it was the verbal inspiration of the Bible and inerrancy that became the storm center of the conflict between the liberals and what we now know as the fundamentalists.

The exact contents of the various lists are not nearly as important as the fact that a major division had taken place in Protestant theological ranks based on how people should relate to the changing intellectual and social environment.

As might be expected, Seventh-day Adventism had historically identified with the conservatives on all the points listed above except that of verbal and inerrant inspiration, neither of which the Bible explicitly teaches. In 1883 the denomination officially rejected verbal inspiration at its General Conference session. The resolution read: "We believe the light given by God to His servants is by the enlightenment of the mind, thus imparting the thoughts, and not (except in rare cases) the very words in which the ideas should be expressed" (RH, Nov. 27, 1883). Ellen White held the same position. In 1886 she wrote that "it is not the words of the Bible that are inspired, but the men that were inspired. Inspiration acts not on the man's words or his expressions but on the man himself, who, under the influence of the Holy Ghost, is imbued with thoughts" (1SM 21). She also rejected the view of inerrancy (that the Bible can have no factual errors, even in details) set forth by the fundamentalists (on this point see my *Reading Ellen White,* pp. 105-112). On the other hand, she had absolutely no doubt as to the divine inspiration of the entire Bible. To her it was God's authoritative word.

With the major exception of the verbal and inerrant nature of inspiration, Ellen White was in essential harmony with the conservatives as they struggled with the liberals' new ideas. She was especially firm on the sinner's hopelessness outside of Christ. Speaking to the liberal agenda on the point of human improvement and goodness, she wrote that "education, culture, the exercise of the will, human effort, all have their proper sphere, but here they are powerless. They may produce an outward correctness of behavior, but they cannot change the heart; they cannot purify the springs of life. There must be a power working from within, a new life from above, before men can be changed from sin to holiness. That power is Christ. His grace alone can quicken the lifeless faculties of the soul, and attract it to God, to holiness"

(SC 18). For Ellen White, Christ was not primarily an example but a Saviour who "suffered the death which was ours, that we might receive the life which was His" (DA 25). She placed herself firmly in the cross-centered conservative camp in the area of sin and salvation.

THE HOLINESS REVIVAL

Beyond the developing controversy between liberal and conservative Protestants and the prominence of D. L. Moody in mass evangelism, the late nineteenth century also saw the rise of the holiness churches, while the first years of the twentieth century witnessed the advent of modern Pentecostalism.

The holiness revival finds its roots in the Wesleyan and Oberlin interests in perfection during the years before the Civil War (discussed in chapter 4). The war shattered the momentum of the earlier movement, but we find it resurrected in 1867 with the founding of the National Campmeeting Association for the Promotion of Holiness. The leaders of the association believed that the teaching of Christian perfection was not receiving adequate exposure in mainline Methodism and other denominations. As a result, they began sponsoring summer camp meetings to provide that emphasis. Before long they also developed the National Publishing Association for the Promotion of Holiness and a foreign missionary organization. Thus the movement began to take on some of the attributes of a denomination.

While the leadership in the national holiness movement was generally Methodist, the regional holiness movements had less Methodist influence, tended to be more independent in their denominational orientation, and often functioned as quasi-churches. By the 1880s and 1890s large numbers of holiness advocates had become alienated from their churches and a strong "come-outism" impulse developed as many holiness leaders advocated the establishment of independent holiness churches in which they could freely teach their emphasis on the Holy Spirit and perfection while at the same time avoiding the drift toward theological liberalism infecting Methodism and other mainline denominations. In many ways the holiness advocates saw themselves as moving back to the "old-time religion."

Eventually several new denominations grew out of the holiness movement. Foremost among them were the Church of the Nazarene and the Church of God (Anderson, Indiana). In addition, some already established religious bodies, such as the Salvation Army and the Free Methodist Church, adopted holiness teachings.

Foremost among those teachings was entire sanctification, often referred to as Christian perfection, the second blessing, full salvation, or the higher Christian life. Many regarded entire sanctification or perfection as a second work of grace. If God's first work in a believer's life was justification by faith, His second was entire sanctification by faith. Some held the second blessing to be instantaneous and dramatic. They believed that entire sanctification or perfection was not an accomplishment but a gift received through surrender.

With the movement's emphasis on the work of the Holy Spirit in a believer's life, a large portion of holiness leaders also emphasized faith healing and other gifts of the Spirit. Some went so far as to claim that Christ had atoned for all sickness at the cross and that the only reason individuals weren't healed was that they lacked faith. By the turn of the century some holiness advocates had begun to emphasize speaking in tongues as a confirmation of the Spirit's work. That emphasis led to the birth of the modern Pentecostal movement.

Seventh-day Adventists were not ignorant of developments in the holiness movement. For example, Hannah Whitall Smith's *Christian's Secret of a Happy Life* was referred to at the 1893 General Conference session by A. T. Jones, advertised in the *Review and Herald,* and marketed by both North American Adventist publishing houses. Beyond that, Jones indicated in 1898 that he approved of many of the leading British holiness movement's ideas on Christian living. Jones, W. W. Prescott, J. N. Loughborough, and other Adventists also got involved in faith healing during the early 1890s in parallel fashion to the movement developing among the holiness advocates. By the turn of the century some Adventists in their "holy flesh" enthusiasm even moved to the fringes of creating their own version of Pentecostalism.

Ellen White was also aware of the holiness teachings of her day. While she commended their emphasis on salvation in Jesus, she decried their demeaning of the law of God (RH, Aug. 13, 1889). In addition, as pointed out in chapter 4, she opposed those teachings of the holiness advocates that indicated that entire sanctification or perfection was an instantaneous work of the Holy Spirit or that Christians could be conscious of their perfection. In a similar manner, she rejected faith healing extremes in both Adventism and the holiness movement. For her, God healed only according to His will. Thus the failure of a person to receive healing did not necessarily imply a lack of faith on his or her part (see letter 93, 1892).

THE SECOND WAVE OF PROTESTANT MISSIONS

Kenneth Scott Latourette has rightly referred to the nineteenth century as the "great century" of Protestant missions. Mission expansion came in two phases. As we saw in chapter 2, the first phase was a by-product of the Second Great Awakening. During the first half of the century India, Burma, Ceylon, West Africa, the Turkish empire, and Hawaii were the chief targets of American missions. By the end of the century the nation would add Latin America and the Orient (especially China) as special fields of interest as American missions spread to every corner of the globe.

The second great wave of nineteenth-century missions would crest in the 1890s and carry over into the early decades of the twentieth century. At the very time that American commercial, political, and economic interests were being extended to various parts of the world, the American churches began to focus more intensely on the needs of people beyond its borders.

Josiah Strong in 1885 in his *Our Country* summoned the American church to assume its full responsibility for Christianizing the world. Strong argued that American ideals rather than its national power should be the focal point of concern in the nation's relationship to other countries. According to Strong "the door of opportunity is open in all the earth. . . . The triumph of the kingdom awaits only the exercise of the power committed to the church." He firmly believed that "it is fully in the hands of the Christians in the United States, during the next ten or fifteen years, to hasten or retard the coming of Christ's kingdom in the world by hundreds, and perhaps thousands, of years."

Strong's appeal fell onto fertile ground. The next year the Student Volunteer Movement for Foreign Missions was born when Dwight L. Moody appealed at a Christian collegiate convention for students to devote their lives to mission service. One hundred took their stand. That number increased to 2,200 in 1887 and to more than 5,000 in 1888. Within a few years many thousands had pledged their lives to mission service. The movement's thrust was that "all should go to all," and its motto was "the evangelization of the world in this generation." The movement stimulated, claims historian Ernest R. Sandeen, "the greatest demonstration of missionary interest ever known in the United States." As Sydney Ahlstrom put it, "the closing two decades of the nineteenth century witnessed the climactic phase of the foreign missions movement in American Protestantism."

Enthusiasm for missions didn't limit itself to North America, even though the United States took the leading role. The 1890s saw major mission programs in Great Britain and in many of the continental nations of Europe.

Seventh-day Adventism was poised to ride the crest of this second wave of mission expansion. In 1886 the denomination had published its first book on foreign missions—*Historical Sketches of the Foreign Missions of the Seventh-day Adventists.* Then in 1889 the denomination sent S. N. Haskell and Percy T. Magan on a two-year itinerary around the world to survey the opportunities, problems, and possible mission sites that awaited Adventist missions in various parts of Africa, India, and the Orient. They fully reported their tour to the church through the pages of the *Youth's Instructor.* Thus missions and mission service began to capture the hearts and minds of Adventist youth in a manner similar to the way the student movement affected thousands of young people in the larger Protestant world. By the end of the 1890s Adventism had established itself on every continent and in many island groups.

Ellen White was one of Adventism's foremost promoters of missions. She never tired of urging the church and its members to sacrifice so that they could carry the message of the three angels to the far corners of the earth.

NORTHERN MISSIONS TO BLACK AMERICA

Protestant North Americans believed not only that they had a mission to the world but also that they had one to their own nation. One subset of that mission was the post-Civil War work done by Northern Protestants for the recently freed slaves in the Southern states. Even while the war was still in progress the Northern churches had become aware of the needs of the exslaves for food, clothing, work opportunities, shelter, and protection. But their most important need, in the eyes of many Protestants, was education. The great bulk of the Black population was illiterate, since in the decades before the war it had been against the law in most parts of the South to teach slaves to read. In the wake of the conflict the Northern churches established nearly 80 agencies to rectify the problem.

Thousands of poorly paid missionaries went south to help educate the 4 million former slaves. While most of these missionaries were quite sincere, many of them were less than diplomatic in their relations with the recently defeated Southern Whites and less than enlightened in their pedagogical techniques. Coupled with those imported problems was the natural hostility of a White population recently overrun militarily and now being invaded culturally.

The result was that Northern missionaries faced hostility and harassment on a regular basis and periodic violence from the rougher elements among the Whites. Part of the opposition to the missionary-teachers rose from a determination to keep the Blacks "in their place." "He is and must continue to be," declared the New Orleans *Christian Advocate* in 1867, "the laboring man of the

South, because he is not fitted . . . for anything higher."

Gradually the magnitude of the task, the ongoing hostility of Southern Whites, and the decline of fervor among leaders of the denominational agencies caused many of the projects to be abandoned. By the mid-1870s the mission to the ex-slaves was in rapid retreat. Nevertheless a beginning had been made, and such institutions as Hampton Institute, Fisk University, Morehouse College, and Atlanta University remained as a heritage of the mission to the freed slaves of the South.

The Seventh-day Adventist Church was a latecomer to the mission to the South. The main reason was not that the denomination had no interest in the problems of the ex-slave in the late 1860s and early 1870s, but rather that it was in its own infancy and preoccupied with its own survival.

The neglect of the "Southern work," as the work for the Blacks in the South came to be labeled in Adventist circles, halted in the 1890s. The stimulus for interest in the topic came from a talk by Ellen White to the denomination's leadership in 1891 entitled "Our Duty to the Colored People." "Sin," she told them, "rests upon us as a church because we have not made greater effort for the salvation of souls among the colored people. . . . White men and White women should be qualifying themselves to work among the colored people. There is a large work to be done in educating this ignorant and downtrodden class" (SW 15, 16).

That appeal fell on deaf ears. But two years later it came into the hands of Ellen White's son Edson, then in the midst of a personal religious awakening. He felt convicted that God was calling him to work among the Black population of the Deep South. The result was his sailing of the *Morning Star* to the Yazoo River region of Mississippi, where he established a vigorous educational/evangelistic/publishing ministry for the Black population. In spite of serious opposition, his work took hold and spread. In 1895 Edson formed the Southern Missionary Society to guide a developing network of self-supporting missions. That same year the denomination formally entered the work for Southern Blacks when it purchased the land for what would be established as the

Oakwood Industrial School in 1896 (now Oakwood College).

Thus far in our examination of the post-Civil War world of Ellen White we have surveyed the social and intellectual changes that took place, the millennial expectations of the times, and some of the religious trends that formed the milieu in which she lived and ministered. We have noted that she was in touch with those times, even though she may not have been in harmony with all of the developing ideas and movements. In chapter 9 we will examine several of the social issues that reformers confronted in the late nineteenth and early twentieth centuries. We will also briefly note Ellen White's relationship to those issues.

Chapter Nine

Social Issues

In chapter 3 we noted that the decades prior to the Civil War were years of reform. The 1820s and 1830s saw a vast array of voluntary societies formed to strike out nearly every conceivable evil and thus bring about heaven on earth or, for those less religiously inclined, at least make our world a better place to live. By the 1850s, however, one issue above all others influenced the passions of the reformers—the freeing of the slaves. That reform drained off the energies and means that had sustained the broad-based agenda of earlier years.

The post-Civil War years, with emancipation accomplished, witnessed the rise of a new array of reforms as idealists continued to strive to "make things right." Although many of the reforms were the same, new emphases would arise and new configurations of reformers would evolve to agitate them.

THE TEMPERANCE MOVEMENT

If one reform above others caught the imagination and energies of the late-nineteenth-century reformers it was abstinence from alcohol. Like the move to free the slaves, temperance became a virtual crusade. And like the abolitionist movement, the temperance crusade would climax in a national event—the passing of the Eighteenth Amendment to the United States Constitution in 1919, prohibiting the sale or manufacture of intoxicating liquors.

The population of the United States in the nineteenth century divided roughly into two parts along the line of attitudes toward alcoholic beverages—some were for them while others regarded them as the foundation of crime and pauperism. The drawing on page 108 reflects that latter position. In it the artist places the blame for much of society's problems on the dealers in alcohol. The problem not only was disruptive in society as a whole, but also devastated the home. A Chicago slum dweller remarked to social worker Jane Addams that "you might say it's a disgrace to have your son beat you up for the sake of a bit of money you've earned scrubbing, but I haven't the heart to blame the boy for doing what he's seen his father do all his life; his father forever went wild when the drink was in him and struck me to the very day of his death."

The temperance movement in the United States went through three stages. The first took place before the Civil War and climaxed with Maine and at least nine other states passing total abstinence laws. By 1865, however, legislatures and courts had repealed or declared most of those laws unconstitutional (see chapter 3).

The second phase of the movement began in 1869 with the organization of the national Prohibition Party. But the real power in this phase was not the political party but the Women's Christian Temperance Union (WCTU). The WCTU grew out of a women's anti-drinking crusade that swept across New York and central Ohio in the winter of 1873-1874. The main technique of the crusade was the "pray-in." Claiming the power of the Holy Spirit, groups of women prayed on barroom floors until the owners agreed to close their establishments. By this method they managed to shut down some 250 saloons in 50 days. Unfortunately, most of the establishments soon reopened. But the idea undergirding the crusade was not lost: *Women could make a difference.*

Under the leadership of Frances E. Willard for the last two decades of the century, the WCTU became a powerful influence in the battle against alcohol. The WCTU not only fought on the temperance front, but also campaigned for other reforms, espe-

HARPER'S WEEKLY

Praying down a saloon

cially women's rights. The WCTU was not only the largest temperance organization before 1900 but also the largest women's organization in the United States up to that time. It provided women with the opportunity to exert their political influence. But influence was not enough for Willard. She contended that only the right to vote would give women power to eliminate alcohol and protect the home.

The third stage of the temperance movement arrived in 1895 with the forming of the Anti-Saloon League of America. Unlike Willard's WCTU, the league had only one aim—the destruction of the saloon. "The Anti-Saloon League believes, as an organization," claimed its literature, "that if we get rid of the saloons, we could trust time, and education, and the spread of morality and religions to discourage and remove whatever private use of liquor as a beverage there may be."

The main agent in performing the league's work was the church. It was the last great crusade that found Protestant liberals and conservatives working together toward a common cause.

By 1913 the league realized that merely getting rid of saloons was not enough. Thenceforth it campaigned for an amendment to the Constitution to prohibit the manufacture or

Placing the weight of crime and pauperism where it should be—on the backs of saloonkeepers

Drunkenness was branded as the cause "of nine tenths of the misery of the working class."

sale of intoxicating beverages. Victory, as we noted earlier, came in 1919 with the adoption of the Eighteenth Amendment.

The Adventist Church and Ellen White were quite active in the temperance movement. The earliest Adventists to hold political office were temperance candidates. And Ellen White penned in 1881 that "the advocates of temperance fail to do their whole duty unless they exert their influence by precept and example— by voice and pen and vote—in favor of prohibition and total abstinence" (RH, Nov. 8, 1881).

Ellen White addressed some of her largest audiences on behalf of temperance. For example, at the Groveland, Massachusetts, camp meeting in 1876 she estimated that some 20,000 attended her temperance lectures. The next year at Groveland she had a repeat performance. The Haverhill *Daily Bulletin* for August 27 commented on the Sunday meeting: "The great occasion of the day was the afternoon service. The trains from all directions had brought immense crowds upon the ground, and the grove literally swarmed with people. Mrs. White spoke on the subject of Christian temperance. This lady is a forcible and impressive speaker, and holds the crowd with her clear utterances and convincing logic."

HEALTH CONCERNS

The Good Old Days—They Were Terrible! The title of Otto Bettmann's pictorial social history of nineteenth-century America was nowhere truer than in the area of health. Even though the early-nineteenth-century health reform movement had achieved some advances, the post-Civil War years were still a time of sanitary, medical, and dietary ignorance. The next six decades, however, would see unprecedented progress in every health-related field.

It is difficult for most Americans today to grasp the fragility of life in the nineteenth century. Not only was infant mortality high, but epidemics and other disasters occurred on a level almost beyond comprehension. The Memphis, Tennessee, yellow fever epidemic of 1878, for example, took 5,150 lives from a population of 38,500. That same year New Orleans lost an estimated

A returning father finds his family stricken with yellow fever.

3,977 to yellow fever. But that was only half as many deaths as the city's 1853 epidemic, which cost 7,848 lives. People attributed yellow fever and other epidemics to bad air—what the authorities called "miasma." Meanwhile, something as basic as a heat wave could cause 3,000 deaths in New York City in 1896.

The sanitary front also left much to be desired. On New York City streets at the turn of the century, for example, horses deposited an estimated 2.5 million pounds of manure and 60,000 gallons of urine daily. And horses were just the beginning of the problem. Only a tiny fraction of houses had indoor toilets. The olfactory and sanitary implications of that fact is incomprehensible to us moderns. The nation's leading public health expert of the 1880s noted that the most annoying nuisance connected with urbanization was the prevalence of the privy, "a single one of [which] may render life in a whole neighborhood almost unendurable in summer." H. L. Menken put it much more bluntly when he remarked that Baltimore in the 1880s smelled "like a billion polecats." The Chicago *Times* described that city as a "solid stink." "No other word expresses it so well as stink," the paper observed. "A stench means something finite. Stink reaches the infinite and becomes sublime in the magnitude of odiousness."

Add uncollected street garbage, polluted water, industrial pollution, and myriads of flies, mosquitoes, roaches, and other insects to the mix, and you have an unenviable mess to say the least. In the absence of underground sewers, many urban rivers and creeks were nothing less than open cesspools.

City housing also left much to be desired. Overcrowding (sometimes a thousand people per city block), poorly ventilated,

CORBIS

The good old days weren't all that good, in terms of sanitation.

apartments (many without even a single window), and unpurified drinking water (even for the wealthy) made cities in themselves health hazards.

Rural life wasn't all that healthy either. Most farms were subsistence operations. And while we might imagine the late-nineteenth-century farmhouse surrounded by a neat rose garden, it is probably more accurate to visualize, as Bettmann points out, "an expanse of muck and manure" circling the dwelling, "sucking at boots and exuding a pestilential stench that attracted swarms of flies, ticks and worms to amplify the miseries of man and beast." Practical purposes dictated that the well be close to the farmhouse, which itself was close to the barnyard, outhouse, stable, pigsty, and chicken coop. One could trace a great deal of the sickness and unexplained "misery" of country dwellers to polluted wells. But the inhabitants sensed no danger. It wasn't until the 1890s that people generally recognized the danger to health posed by dirty drinking water. Sanitary preparation and storage of food also left much to be desired in both rural and urban America during the post-Civil War years.

Beyond general sanitation, personal health habits and medical knowledge also needed improvement in the decades after 1865. In 1882 only an estimated 2 percent of the homes in New York City had water connections. Bathing for most people was a rarity. Advocacy of the Saturday night bath was no joke. It was a revolutionary practice advocated by health reformers. In 1872 when Ellen White recommended that "persons in health" should "bathe as often as twice a week" (3T 70), she was on the cutting edge of an aspect of personal health care. Inadequate and poorly balanced diets also created health problems in the last half of the nineteenth century.

Moreover, medical care was still problematic, as it had been in the antebellum years. The United States had only about 200 hospitals during the 1870s, and more than a third of those were for the mentally deranged. In the post-Civil War decades hospitals more closely resembled almshouses for the poor than today's health-care institutions. Because of the total absence of hygiene, they were generally deathtraps. Those in better financial condition either had themselves treated at home or went to spas or health reform sanitariums for rest and recuperation. A society woman who visited New York's Bellevue Hospital in 1872 confessed that she had previously hardly known hospitals existed. Of her visit she reported: "The loathsome smell sickened me. The condition of the beds and patients was unspeakable. The one nurse slept in the bathroom and the tub was filled with filthy rubbish."

Even the term *nurse* didn't mean what it does today. The nation had no nurses' training until Bellevue opened the first program in 1873. Many so-called nurses were drunken women given hospital duty in lieu of a prison sentence.

Training for doctors wasn't all that advanced either. It still consisted of a four- to eight-month course. When president Charles Eliot of Harvard sought to initiate written exams for the graduates of Harvard Medical School in 1869, his request was refused because, said the dean, "a majority of the students cannot write well enough." James Edson White and his brother took medical training during this period. Edson quipped of his experience that the physi-

A meat market before the advent of refrigeration

Over-the-counter opium, the poor child's nurse

cian in charge "is a villain—the Hygieo-Therapeutic Clinic is a humbug, and the Old Doctor Mill ought to be tipped into the Delaware [River]."

Knowledge and control of drugs was still a problem. While some of the heroic techniques of the prewar period had fallen out of favor, such as purging a patient's system through the use of poisonous drugs (see chapter 3), the use of patent drugs consisting largely of alcohol and containing opium and other narcotics was widespread. Such concoctions sold without prescriptions. Much yet remained to be done in the way of reforming the nation's health care and practices.

That reform would come largely along two lines of development. The first had to do with better private and public health. On the private level the latter part of the nineteenth and early part of the twentieth century witnessed significant improvements in personal hygiene and diet among large sectors of the population. It was in that context that Dr. John Harvey Kellogg in the 1890s launched the prepared breakfast food industry in connection with the Adventists' Battle Creek Sanitarium in Michigan. The final decades of the century also saw more people take an interest in physical fitness.

The public realm witnessed a move to clean up hospitals. Because of better sanitation, improved medical education, and advances in medical science, hospitals by the turn of the century were becoming places where sick people could actually go to get well.

Also in the public arena were the development of municipal water and sewer systems and the initiation of regular garbage pickup. Such projects often had a government origin. During these years the government also took a proactive stance in public health by creating boards of health to inspect schools, hospitals, and food handlers, as well as to perform other tasks. The Progressive movement in politics also engineered legislation to establish agencies to set standards for such industries as those dealing in food and drugs. The development of refrigeration and pasturization bettered dietary health. In short, vast improvements toward better health took place in the late nineteenth century.

The same period provided significant advances in medical care. Two discoveries in particular made them possible. The first concerned the acceptance of the germ theory. Lacking an understanding of germs, physicians not using clean instruments or even washing their hands between patients had often done more to spread disease than to cure it. Antiseptic procedures were absolutely crucial for the development of safe hospitals and routinely successful surgical procedures.

The second major discovery that changed the nature of medical practice had to do with anesthesia. Pain-deadening anesthesia meant that surgeons were no longer compelled to complete an operation in a matter of seconds or minutes. Their new freedom opened the way for procedures never before attempted. The use of antiseptics and anesthesia made it possible for surgeons to operate successfully in such areas as the abdomen, skull, and chest.

The first decades of the twentieth century also witnessed the professionalization of medical education. More than half of the existing medical schools in the United States were forced to close down while those that survived were upgraded.

It was during these years that the Seventh-day Adventist Church established the College of Medical Evangelists (now Loma Linda University). Because of the problem of rising standards and costs, some of the denomination's leaders wanted to make the school into a paramedical institution, but Ellen White argued for an institution that provided a complete medical education that led to the graduation of fully qualified individuals in the science of modern medicine. As she put it, "the medical school at Loma Linda is to be of the highest order." The youth were to receive "a medical education that will enable them to pass the examinations required by law of all who practice as regularly qualified physicians" (MM 57).

Ellen White was not only in harmony with the advances in medical and nursing training, but also in general agreement with the developments in both public and private health. In many ways such advances were culminations of ideas and practices that she had argued for before 1865, which we surveyed in chapter 3.

EDUCATIONAL DEVELOPMENTS

As in the field of health, the world of education went through a thorough transformation between 1865 and 1915. Once again, many of the changes resulted from reforms begun before the Civil War (see chapter 3).

One of the most significant changes had to do with the rise of science. Prior to the 1850s the classical languages and literatures had dominated secondary and collegiate education. But that domination would be challenged in the wake of Darwinism's ascendancy.

British philosopher Herbert Spencer heralded the coming battle when he confronted the educational world in 1854 with its most provocative question: "What knowledge is of most worth?" To Spencer that was the question of questions. "Before there can be a rational *curriculum,"* he penned, "we must settle which things it most concerns us to know; . . . we must determine the relative value of knowledges." For Spencer the answer was obvious—"science" was the most valuable knowledge for every field of human endeavor.

Not everyone agreed with Spencer's conclusion. The curricular battle spanning the last half of the nineteenth century found varying answers to his all-important question. Some continued to hold that the classics were the knowledge of most value, since their study developed mental power and provided the knowledge that defined the educated person. Others suggested that the knowledge of most import was vocational.

The stakes were high in that curricular struggle. The winner would shape the minds of the coming generation. Ellen White did not remain aloof from the strife. She flatly rejected the position of those who opted for the classics, science, or vocational knowledge as the dominating center of the curriculum. She unequivocally held that the Bible lies "at the foundation of all education worthy of the name" (FE 448). "The science of redemption is the science of all sciences." Its study "will quicken the mind and uplift the soul" (Ed 126) because it calls "the highest faculties of the human mind . . . into intense activity" (Ed 124). "Higher education," she argued, "is an experimental [i.e., experiential] knowledge of the plan of salvation, and this knowledge is secured by earnest and diligent study of the Scriptures. Such an education will renew the mind and transform the character, restoring the image of God in the soul" (CT 11).

Throughout the last two decades of the nineteenth century Ellen White would lead the battle in Adventist education to uproot the classics from their position of dominance and establish the Bible and its philosophy at the very center of the curriculum. A similar struggle took place among the nation's colleges and secondary schools. By the end of the century the hegemony of the classics had shattered nearly everywhere. In the public sector the scientific, technological, and vocational fields had displaced the classics, while in Adventist schools the study of the Bible was well on its way toward achieving its rightful curricular position.

Schools at all levels were also healthier places, students had more of a mental and physical balance, and teaching techniques had become much more effective. Thus some of the reform impulses of the 1820s and 1830s found fulfillment by the end of the century.

Before moving away from the topic of education, we should examine the response of the conservative wing of Protestantism to the new directions in higher education. Those developing into premillennial fundamentalists became disenchanted with both the Darwinian direction of public institutions and by the higher biblical criticism and "apostate scholarship" tainted with evolutionary ideas that occupied an ever larger place in Christian colleges and seminaries.

Their response was the Bible institute movement. The first Bible institute was Nyack Missionary College, founded in New York in 1883 as the Missionary Training College for Home and Foreign Missionaries and Evangelists. The second such institution was the Moody Bible Institute, begun in 1886.

The aim of the missionary colleges and Bible institutes was to prepare for mission service Christian young people "who have neither means nor the time to attend college and seminary." As such, these schools avoided academic degrees and tended to be subcollegiate. The missionary college/Bible institute movement grew in response to the continued drift toward liberalism of many Protestant colleges and seminaries and by the enthusiasm generated by the Student Volunteer Movement for "the evangelization of the world in this generation."

The 1890s and early 1900s also saw several Adventist institutions rise with "missionary college" as part of their title. As with the fundamentalist schools, their names were a response to a heightened sense of world mission.

Ellen White, as might be expected, shared many of the goals of the Bible institute/missionary college movement, but she guided Adventist higher education toward a more moderate position. She counseled toward a more balanced approach in which students studied "the sciences and at the same time . . . [learned]

the requirements of His Word" (5T 21). After the turn of the century she urged Adventist colleges to offer "all that is essential for entrance into a medical college" in line with the various state laws (CT 479, 480). Thus she set the direction for Adventist institutions to become fully accredited liberal arts colleges rather than to follow the more restricted path of the Bible institutes. Time has shown that counsel to be essential, since practitioners in many fields (e.g., teaching, nursing, public accounting) must have accredited degrees as a prerequisite to licensing and practice.

RACIAL ISSUES

While many social issues, such as the health field and education, moved toward a better resolution between 1865 and 1915, that was not true in all areas. A case in point was race relations. The freeing of the slaves during the Civil War was only the beginning of a process that would hopefully enable the nation to sort out its race problems. The next few years witnessed some positive advances. Between 1865 and 1870 the United States amended its Constitution to abolish slavery (the Thirteenth Amendment), extend citizenship to Blacks (the Fourteenth Amendment), and give them the right to vote (the Fifteenth Amendment). Beyond that, 1866 and 1875 saw Congress pass two civil rights bills, and in 1865 it set up the Freedman's Bureau to aid the freed slaves as they sought to find their place in American society. Hopeful signs appeared on the horizon in spite of continuing racial tensions between Southerners of the two races and between Southerners and those Northern Whites who were aggravating a difficult situation. The Blacks in the Southern states even managed to send 17 of their number, including two senators, to Congress before 1900.

What appeared to be progress, however, met with a major reversal beginning with the end of Reconstruction in 1877. At that point recently elected President Rutherford B. Hayes agreed to leave the South alone to work out its racial problem without interference from the federal government. The next 30 years brought about a rapid decline in Black rights. In 1883 the Supreme Court nullified that part of the 1875 Civil Rights Act that barred discrimination in public places and on public carriers. Seven years earlier the Court had sharply curtailed the protection afforded Blacks under the Fifteenth Amendment.

The 1890s witnessed a radical turn for the worse. By 1890 the new waves of immigration had fanned the flames of nativism, emotions that fed a growing racism in the nation as a whole. In that year the Supreme Court ruled that a state could require segregation on public carriers. Six years later the Court in *Plessy v. Ferguson* opened the future to segregation of all kinds with its "separate but equal" doctrine. By 1910 racial segregation was mandated in federal office buildings in the nation's capital. By that time the majority of people in all regions accepted segregation.

The 1890s also saw concerted efforts to keep Blacks from voting. Through such avenues as poll taxes and literacy tests every Southern state found a way to disenfranchise Black voters legally. Thus in Louisiana, where there had been 130,344 registered Black voters in 1896, only 5,320 remained in 1900 and 1,342 in 1904. In Alabama registered Black voters dropped from a high of 181,471 to 3,000 in 1900.

Black education had also reached a crisis point. In 1890 only 20 percent of all Black children received any education at all. Governor James Kimball Vardaman of Mississippi declared in the early twentieth century that any money spent on Black education was "a robbery of the white man."

The philosophic base of much of the racism and nativism of the day was that of social Darwinism. Even most of those friendly to Blacks had been indoctrinated with an evolutionary racial hierarchy that graded the races by placing Caucasians at the top of the evolutionary scale and the African at the bottom. People had used such conceptions to justify slavery in the antebellum period and racial discrimination thereafter. Most Whites believed in Black inferiority as a scientific fact.

Ellen White rejected that point of view. She held that the apparent and real deficiencies of the Blacks of her time resulted from slavery and subsequent oppression. "Many," she claimed, "have had no chance who might have manifested decided ability if they had been blessed with opportunities such as their more favored brethren, the white people, have had" (letter 80a, 1895). She also argued that "every effort should be made to wipe out the terrible wrong which has been done them" (SW 15).

WOMEN'S RIGHTS

Another of the several "liberation" movements that would eventuate in a constitutional amendment was the drive for women's rights. As we noted in chapter 3, the early crusaders for female rights compared their condition to the bondage of the slaves. As abolitionist Lydia Maria Child put it: "Cursed is that system of considering human beings as chattel! Whether it be because they are women, or because they are colored." Such feelings did not lessen when after the Civil War the federal government not only excluded women from the provisions of the Fourteenth and Fifteenth Amendments (having to do with the right of Blacks to vote), but raised the issue of whether women were actually citizens by including the word "male" in the Fourteenth Amendment.

In 1869 both the National Woman Suffrage Association and the less militant American Woman Suffrage Association organized. The leaders of the first association were Elizabeth Cady

Crusaders for women's rights: Elizabeth Cady Stanton and Susan B. Anthony, about 1870

Stanton and Susan B. Anthony. Lucy Stone headed the second. The two groups merged in 1890.

Women first won the right to vote in Wyoming Territory in 1869. That right remained intact when Wyoming achieved statehood in 1890. Colorado (1893), Utah (1896), and Idaho (1896) rapidly followed. But in spite of such victories the woman's movement was unsuccessful in getting a woman suffrage amendment even though they tried annually from 1870 on. That victory would not take place until 1920, with the adoption of the Nineteenth Amendment. Women finally had the rights of full citizens as defined for Black males in the Fourteenth and Fifteenth Amendments.

Meanwhile, women had, as we noted earlier in this chapter, flexed their muscles in the temperance movement. In fact, under the leadership of Frances E. Willard, the Woman's Christian Temperance Union fought almost as much for female rights and the right to vote as it did for temperance.

Two other areas of change for females in the late nineteenth century were education and the workplace. The second half of the century found more colleges opening their doors to women on an equal basis with men. In addition, all-female collegiate institutions developed. Vassar in 1865 was the first. Several of the institutions eventually offered first-rate educations.

Most females who entered the workplace did so at the lower levels, but others managed to break into the professions. In 1849 Elizabeth Blackwell graduated from medical school, in 1852 Antoinette Brown was ordained to the ministry, and in 1869 Arabella Mansfield was the first female admitted to a state bar to practice law. Step by step women gained ground in terms of their rights, but much of it came only after a great deal of effort and pain.

Ellen White was not oblivious to such struggles. She had no doubt that God had created women as the equal of men, but she never felt it her mission to campaign in the woman's rights movement. While she seems to have been in harmony with its general aims, she definitely disagreed with the lifestyles of some of the movement's leading advocates.

That didn't mean that she took a back seat in the male-dominated world in which she lived. To the contrary, she assumed a prominent (yet unofficial) leadership role in guiding the Adventist Church, and did not back away from confronting dominating males when she felt it her duty. Beyond her personal involvement, she encouraged other females to spread the Adventist message. Women gospel workers, she noted, "are just as greatly needed to do the work to which He has appointed them as are men" (Ev 493).

CAPITAL AND LABOR

The recent industrialization of the nation brought stresses and strains of a type and magnitude not experienced before. While problems between labor and capital existed before the Civil War, those difficulties escalated to unimagined heights in the postwar decades. Not only did such industries as steel and the railroads expand exponentially, but the prevailing laissez-faire doctrine of social Darwinisn served as justification for the privileged classes piling up unparalleled riches at the expense of the hundreds of thousands who worked for them. The "fittest" under this scheme were doing extremely well indeed.

But the working class was in trouble. Many had largely become wage slaves. Although penned in the 1840s, the following observation of journalist Orestes Brownson was even truer a half century later. "The man who employs them," Brownson wrote, "and for whom they are toiling as so many slaves, is one of our city nabobs, reveling in luxury; or he is a member of our legislature, enacting laws to put money in his own pocket; or he is a member of Congress, contending for a high tariff to tax the poor for the benefit of the rich."

While the reigning capitalists piled up their millions, a workingman might receive only $1-2 for a 12-hour day, women got less, and young children as little as $2 a week. And workers didn't receive much pity. Horsecar drivers in New York City received $12 a week for six 16-hour days. State Assemblyman Teddy Roosevelt in the early 1880s branded as "communistic" their demand for a 12-hour day.

Child labor was inexpensive for employers but dangerous and debilitating to children.

Without workers' compensation, injured workers had to return to work or starve.

Not only was pay low and hours long, but working conditions were notoriously unsafe. In order to achieve maximum production, factories deliberately set machinery at the utmost speed at which a worker could operate. Meanwhile, protective devices were practically nonexistent. Otto Bettmann notes that in 1890 one railroad worker was killed for every 306 employed and one out of every 30 was injured. "Out of a work force of 749,301 this amounted to a yearly total of 2,451 deaths, which rose in 1900 to 2,675 killed and 41,142 injured." Mining was even worse. Social commentators said that the miner "went down to work as to an open grave, not knowing when it might close on him."

And what did the injured worker receive in compensation? Virtually nothing, except burial if killed on the job. Bettmann points out that "whether a worker was mutilated by a buzz saw, crushed by a beam, interred in a mine, or fell down a shaft, it was always 'his own bad luck." The courts generally always ruled for the employer. On top of that, there was no such thing as Social Security, workers' compensation, or other legislated protection for disabled workers and their families. An injured worker was without rights and his family left destitute. And why, we might ask, did industrial workers accept such conditions? Because they had no choice if they wanted to feed their families.

Not only were wages low, but they could get worse real quick. The Pullman Company crisis in 1894 is a good example. In the midst of severe economic depression the company discharged 4,000 of its 5,800 employees and drastically cut the wages of its remaining workers. Meanwhile, company rent remained the same, as did prices in the company-owned stores. That was serious, since Pullman literally owned the community the workers lived and shopped in. In the meantime, regular dividends went out to the well-to-do investors who owned shares in the company.

Workers didn't have a lot of options when it came to settling their grievances. But one thing was certain: individual workers had no hope of successfully negotiating with large corporations. Companies merely replaced the disgruntled employees if they exposed their grievances. Beyond that, employers could use a "lockout" to starve workers into submission, and they could call on the federal courts with their well-fed judges to back them up.

The only option that seemed to hold much chance of success was unionization in the hope of creating a monopoly of labor that could successfully do business with the monopoly of capital. That solution, as might be expected given the financial stakes at issue, resulted in violence.

One of the few ways that organized labor could make itself heard was through the stoppage of work—the labor strike. Some 23,798 labor strikes took place between 1880 and 1900 involving more than 6 million workers. About half ended in failure and another 15 percent in compromise. Unfortunately, physical violence and the destruction of property accompanied some of the strikes. The employers, meanwhile, felt fully justified in compounding the problem by using violence to counter the strikes.

They hired private armies and utilized government troops to keep rowdies in line.

The Protestant churches generally took the side of capital against labor. Henry Ward Beecher said of strikers: "If the club of the policeman, knocking out the brains of the rioter, will answer, then well and good; but if it does not promptly meet the exigency, then bullets and bayonets, canister and grape . . . constitute the one remedy. . . . Napoleon was right when he said the way to deal with a mob is to exterminate it." While that statement may have been extreme for a clergyman, it did express the mentality behind

Destruction of railway depot: Frustrated workers at times fought unfair labor practices with violence.

much of the practice of the day when it came to strikebreaking.

The religious issue became more prominent in the capital versus labor issue when the Roman Catholic Church entered on the side of labor. In 1891 Pope Leo XIII issued his encyclical *Rerum Novarum,* in which he deplored the dehumanization of workers by unrestrained capitalism. Many Protestants came to see unioniza-

Labor violence was a two-way street. Employers at times hired private armies, and at other times used Federal troops to control workers.

tion as either a plot by European socialists to ruin the country or as a move by Catholicism to destroy it. Thus emotions ran high along several lines in the struggle between capital and labor.

Ellen White saw the capital versus labor conflict in terms of the last days. Not only did she quote James 5:1, 3-6 in faulting the capitalists for their "greed and oppression" in keeping down the workers (PK 651), but she saw that oppressive unions would be *"one* of the agencies that will bring upon this earth a time of trouble such as has not been since the world began" (2SM 142; italics supplied). She didn't see either side as clean. "The wicked," she penned, "are being bound up in bundles, bound up in trusts [the monopolistic businesses of the day], in unions [monopolistic labor], in confederacies" (4BC 1142). She was as much against oppressive business as she was against oppressive labor. Mrs. White opposed oppressive combinations of any sort that would restrict the freedom of Christians to serve God. But she really saw no complete solution to the root problem of the labor versus capital struggle (selfishness) short of the second coming of Christ.

SABBATH REFORM

Both the Colonies before the American Revolution and the early American republic had tied faithful Sabbath (Sunday) observance to God's covenant promises. Keeping the Lord's day holy meant God's blessing, while desecrating it brought trouble. Furthermore, Sunday faithfulness had strong connections to the nation's millennial mission.

At no time did the nation need God's blessing more than in the Civil War, when it seemed to be under the chastising hand of God. In 1864, at the height of the crisis, a convention of evangelicals launched the National Reform Association. The group had as its goal "to maintain existing Christian features in the American government, and to secure such an amendment to the Constitution of the United States as will indicate that this is a Christian nation, and will place all the Christian laws, institutions, and usages of our government on an undeniable legal basis in the fundamental law of the land."

The National Reform Association and other organizations with similar purposes not only were inspired by their understanding of America's millennial vision, but felt threatened by the hordes of new immigrants with their un-American and un-Protestant ways. The new immigration coming from Southern and Eastern Europe had two traits that especially aroused the fears of old-line Americans. First, they guzzled great amounts of alcoholic beverages, and second, in place of keeping Sunday strictly in the way of the Anglo-American Sabbath, they popularized the "Continental Sunday." "The Continental Sunday," claimed Wilbur Crafts, "means at least half a day of shopkeeping, with some servile labor, and a great deal of noisy amusement and drinking." The Continental Sunday "is more to be feared than the Continental plague." The answer, many Protestants believed, was strict Sunday laws. Thus Sunday legislation joined the Protestant agenda along with the temperance crusade as the na-

LAND, R&H PUBLISHING ASSOCIATION

Some Tennessee Adventists were sentenced to chain gangs for the crime of working on Sunday.

tion sought to maintain its millennial-nation standing in the face of ever-increasing numbers of new immigrants who, they believed, were threatening America's favored-nation status.

The 1880s saw Sunday legislation and persecution grow in strength and scope. The problem surfaced in an explosive way in California in 1882, when the Sunday question became a major issue in the state elections. The consequences of the Sunday agitation hit Adventists when the local authorities arrested W. C. White for operating the Pacific Press on Sunday.

The scene of action shifted from California to Arkansas and Tennessee in the mid-eighties. The authorities arrested several Adventists and some, including ministers, served in chain gangs as common criminals.

Adventist excitement over the issue intensified in 1888 when Roman Catholic Cardinal James Gibbons endorsed a petition to Congress on behalf of national Sunday legislation. The Protestants were more than willing to accept such help. "Whenever they [the Roman Catholics] are willing to cooperate in resisting the progress of political atheism," proclaimed the Protestant *Christian Statesman* in 1884, "we will gladly join hands with them."

The high-water mark in the excitement over the Sunday issue came on May 21, 1888, when New Hampshire's H. W. Blair introduced a bill into the United States Senate to promote the observance of "the Lord's day" as a "day of religious worship."

The Blair bill went down to defeat in 1888 and again in 1889, but the Sunday forces didn't give up. They repeatedly sponsored national Sunday legislation for the next two decades.

Ellen White, along with her fellow believers, saw the Sunday agitation as pointing to the fulfillment of those prophecies that indicated an end-time crisis over the law of God (see Rev. 12:17-14:12). Her fullest response to the issue appeared in the 1888 and 1911 editions of *The Great Controversy*.

THE PROGRESSIVE MOVEMENT

Progressives refers to those reformers who became active around the turn of the century at all levels of government. Early in the movement a coterie of popular writers known as the muckrakers exposed the scandalous conditions in business and politics and called for reform. Their writings, along with those of the Social Gospelers (see chapter 8) and those social Darwinists who held that the human brain had evolved to the place where humans could direct evolutionary development, pushed the Progressive politicians to clean things up. Their influence was partly responsible for the Meat Inspection Act, the Pure Food and Drug Act, and certain moves to break up the power of monopolistic big business.

The Progressive movement would also eventuate in the direct election of senators and the right to vote for women. Thus the reforming impulse of the Progressives not only helped correct abuses, but also sought to make the nation more democratic. In many ways much of the reformist drive of the late nineteenth century came to a head in the Progressive movement of the first two decades of the twentieth century.

Chapter Ten

The New Leisure

Like nearly everything else in the post-Civil War years, the nature of leisure also changed. Perhaps we should say that for the first time leisure was becoming a reality for most people. Prior to that time, only the wealthy had free time, while unremitting work was the lot of the masses. Leisure just didn't exist for most people. With a 70-to 80-hour workweek, no vacation, and only limited activities available on Sunday, life was a constant round of work and activities closely related to work.

Coupled with the no-leisure reality was a philosophy handed down from the Puritan forebears that regarded idleness as a central sin (the sin that opened the way for gambling, drinking, and so on) and work as a central virtue. *The New Englander,* a Congregationalist magazine, set forth the philosophy nicely in 1851: "Let our readers, one and all, remember that we were sent into the world, not for sport and amusement, but for labor; not to enjoy and please ourselves, but to serve and glorify God, and be useful to our fellow men. That is the great object and end of life. In pursuing this end, God has indeed permitted us all needful diversion and recreation. . . . But the great end of life after all is work."

The harnessing of the machine gradually shortened the workweek to 60 hours by the end of the eighties and for many workers to about 50 hours by the turn of the century. Beyond that, many businesses introduced the Saturday half-holiday, Labor Day became a holiday in the early 1890s, and the yearly vacation became a fact of life for the prospering middle class. With less work came leisure and with leisure began the rise of leisure industries (such as sports and entertainment) as we know them in the twentieth century.

The leisure industries were made possible not only by the creation of more free time for more people, but also by urbanization. After all, commercial amusements need a critical mass of patrons if they are to be profitable. In this chapter we will look at two avenues the new leisure took as it expanded its tentacles throughout the social fabric: (1) sports and recreation and (2) entertainment.

SPORTS AND RECREATION

One aspect of the sports revolution had to do with the rise of those team sports that have grown so close to the center of American culture, such as baseball, football, and basketball. All three were "invented" in the second half of the nineteenth century.

The first to gain popularity was baseball. Having begun in the 1850s as a gentleman's game, baseball became a favorite pastime of the Union Army during the Civil War and thus became a sport of the common people. Although purely amateur at first, the pressure to win led to hiring skilled players. By 1869 the Cincinnati Red Stockings had a full roster of salaried players. Their amazing record (58 wins, with one tie and no losses, in 1869) prompted other teams to follow suit. But with finances and success came problems, such as gambling and game fixing. The National League began in 1876 to clean up the game and provide it with respectability. Communities soon constructed large ballparks seating thousands, and the nation entered the era of mass spectator sports.

While baseball ruled in the professional realm, football literally transformed what it meant to be an American college. Princeton and Rutgers played the first intercollegiate game in 1869. Attempts began in the 1880s to clean up the game, but the competitive drive to win at all costs and the hiring of athletes for supposedly amateur contests had shifted football toward brutality.

The Cornell University team had an especially appalling reputation for its aggressiveness. In 1876 both Harvard and Yale refused to play Cornell, yet they were brutal enough themselves. In 1884 the New York *Evening Post* reported a game between Yale and Princeton in which "the spectators could see the eleven hurl themselves together and build themselves into kicking, writhing heaps." Brute strength was the rule of the field, and that without any protective padding and headgear.

In 1905 eighteen Americans died on the collegiate football field. At Harvard the season provided only two games without

Yale versus Princeton: college football often led to injuries and sometimes death.

concussions. A player in a Penn-Swarthmore game that year received such a systematic and thorough beating that his bloodied face became a nationwide photographic sensation. That photo raised the ire of President Theodore Roosevelt, who thundered that if the colleges didn't clean up the sport, he would abolish it by executive order. In the spirit of the Progressive movement that had led Roosevelt to face off with American industrial corporations, the president met with the coaches and directors of several leading college teams and laid the responsibility of reform on them. By 1906 reform was well under way. Today, of course, most universities are better known for their football teams than for their academic respectability or lack thereof.

Beyond the gladiatorial realm of spectator sports, the latter part of the 1800s also witnessed the rise of participatory sports. The interest in improved health not only spawned better sanitary conditions and better eating habits, but also the physical fitness movement. Gymnasiums sprang up in urban areas and on school campuses during the 1880s. Popular outdoor participatory sports were golf, tennis, and archery. But the two that became virtual crazes were croquet and bicycling, although some moralists condemned the former because it exposed feminine ankles and promoted flirtation.

Bicycles became a rage in the early 1890s, and every member of many middle-class families felt that they just had to have one. The problem was that they were expensive—up to six months of a laboring man's salary each. Their use represented not inexpensive transportation but show and keeping up with the Joneses of the day. Bicycling clubs formed, and their members designed uniforms. It became the thing to do, even though it had the slightly disconcerting effect of nearly bankrupting the family. Bicycles, however, did provide good outdoor exercise. Of course, they continued to do so for many after the short-lived fad died and their price became reasonable.

Beyond spectator and participatory sports, late-nineteenth-century recreation had its sports on the seamier side. In this category we find such uplifting pastimes as rat baiting. On a bit higher level were the brutal, bare-knuckle boxing matches of the day. A contest did not end, notes one commentator, "until one man had been at least punched, kicked, and bitten into bloody unconsciousness." The hero of the 1880s was John L. Sullivan, who in 1889 took 75 knockdown rounds in 106-degree heat to

Bicycling became a keeping-up-with-the-Joneses fad in the early 1890s.

Starved rats were set upon each other with heavy betting on prospective survivors.

CORBIS

Boxing became a "school of brutality," with matches lasting up to 75 rounds.

defeat Jake Kilrain. The sport became so murderous that New York City outlawed it. The bowling "saloon" and billiard hall also achieved a growing patronage in the post-Civil War period and soon became hangouts for the rougher sorts. On a more positive side, the progressive period of the early twentieth century also saw the increasing establishment of city parks and playgrounds.

Ellen White had mixed feelings regarding the new recreational environments. She was most against football and boxing, which "have become schools of brutality," and she discouraged such activities in Adventist schools (Ed 210). Also she opposed emphasizing competition, and thought that Christians in their various activities should focus on cooperation. In addition, she enthusiastically advocated that individuals get daily physical exercise, but cautioned against excesses in gymnastic exercises and investing too much of one's enthusiasm in team sports (Ed 210). Her highest recommendation for beneficial exercise was "useful employment" in the "open air" (Ed 215, 219), though she did not condemn the "simple exercise of playing ball." However, she cautioned against overdoing the latter because Christians should have other priorities for their time and money (AH 499).

ENTERTAINMENT

Beyond the realm of sport and recreation, the second half of the nineteenth century also saw development in the entertainment sector. Two areas that are important for this study are those of the popular novel and the theater.

The advance in printing in the first half of the century (see chapter 5) not only provided for the possibility of the penny newspaper and massive amounts of religious and reform literature, but also stimulated the popular book publishing business as it sought to reach the masses.

Popular fiction in the nineteenth century ran along three tracks. The first was the romantic novel, generally written by females for females. Plot-oriented, they focused on such womanly concerns as romantic emotions, marriage, and fashion. The plots centered on young maidens beset by male seducers, with an ending in marriage if the maiden managed to tame her counterpart or in death if she crossed the fence of virtue before marriage. Thus the novels generally included a moral lesson on how to conduct one's personal affairs.

The second category of popular fiction that arose around midcentury aimed at males. The stock-in-trade of the "dime novel" was adventure. The plot often centered on Indian slaughter, crime, and "the bad, bad outlaw." One historian of this literary genre notes that "as to the number of Indians killed, the total must have been many times the total Indian population of the United States."

As with the romantic novel, mass production of dime novels, rather than quality, was the name of the game. Prentiss Ingraham, for example, wrote about 1,000 dime novels—121 on the exploits of Buffalo Bill—even though he did not get started until midlife. John Wood found in his study of late-nineteenth-century fiction that the most successful novels were eventually printed in beautifully embossed and gilded bindings and were

"Put down that novel! It will ruin your soul." Novels were widely condemned in the early nineteenth century, but found wider acceptance in later decades.

considered "high-class" fiction. On the other end of the production process, before their publication as novels these works often appeared as serials in "storypapers" in newspaper format.

A third category of popular fiction was the religious novel, which hoped to overcome "mere" sensationalism and at the same time reach a new audience by importing religious lessons into the plot or by creating the plot around a religious or biblical story. Thus the Reverend Joseph Holt Ingraham (the father of Prentiss) authored the immensely popular *Prince of the House of David* and other stories that his son referred to as "dime novels of the Bible." This approach led Ellen White and some of her contemporaries to condemn religious novels and religious fiction, even though they could recommend the reading of *Pilgrim's Progress,* equally a product of the author's imagination.

The difference between *Pilgrim's Progress* and some of the dime novels of the Bible seems to have been qualitative rather than whether something actually happened in history. The plain fact is that the popular novel industry of the late nineteenth century greatly resembled the soap-opera/prime-time television industry of the late twentieth. A major study of Ellen White's use of the term *fiction* indicates that it applies to works with the following characteristics: "(1) It is addictive. (2) It may be sentimental, or sensational, erotic, profane, or trashy. (3) It is escapist, causing the reader to revert to a dream world and to be less able to cope with the problems of everyday life. (4) It unfits the mind for serious study, and devotional life. (5) It is time consuming and valueless." That description puts Ellen White in harmony with the critics of the sensational literature of her day and with many of the critics of the popular media of our time.

Closely related to the popular novel in terms of quality was the popular theater. Of course, the theater had several difficulties attached to it that went beyond the quality of its performances. Two of them had to do with personalities and environment. As to personalities, the private lives of the actors were hardly the highest models of Victorian morality.

The environment of the theater itself had two problems. One was that nineteenth-century theaters were often located in the part of town with the largest proportion of saloons, billiard halls, and brothels. But the most serious issue in relation to the theater being a spiritually and morally risky *place* is that it had close ties to prostitution. While the lower floors provided an excellent location for the more respectable prostitutes to meet their clients, up into the 1880s the entire gallery, or "third tier," was given over to lower-class prostitutes and their consorts. The third tier even had a separate entrance so that respectable people would not have to encounter these "ladies of the night." It is little wonder that the theater as an evil place found emphasis in much of the Christian evaluation of it.

The content, of course, justly came in for its share of criticism. As with the popular novel, sensationalism, emotionalism, and adventure held center stage. The audience for the melodrama of the day, notes Delmer Davis, "was essentially lower-class, made up of the masses who were being burdened and exploited by the industrial revolution, a group whose lives were often horrible in their day-to-day

NELL'S DANGER.
TOM'S HEROIC SLIDE DOWN THE LUMBER FLUME.

Both the drama and novels of the day focused on sentimental sensationalism.

dinginess and poverty, a group who longed for escape and sentimentally wished for moral justice to repair their own sufferings." As a result, rich people in melodramas were often villains, while a workingman was often the hero who rescued the damsel in distress.

Even though filled with stabbings, shootings, hangings, stranglings, poisonings, suicides, fires, shipwrecks, train wrecks, savage villains, and heroes who experienced a series of fearful domestic and physical agonies, the drama of the day pointed toward a conclusion of ultimate happiness and the triumph of virtue over evil. Needless to say, the action was fast-moving and the plot adventuresome.

As with the sentimental and dime novels, one doesn't have to be too imaginative to see the "stuff" of modern media in the nineteenth-century drama. Of course, today heroes don't have to be virtuous, nor does good necessarily win over evil. But outside of those moralisms not much has changed, except for the form of the media itself.

Beyond drama, the nineteenth-century theater hosted minstrel shows, vaudeville performances, and Shakespearean reproductions.

Ellen White feared for the results of those who indulged in the escapist forms of entertainment prevalent in her times. She saw the theater of her day as "the very hotbed of immorality," a medium that could "deprave the imagination and debase the morals," "destroy religious impressions," and "blunt the relish for the tranquil pleasures and sober realities of life" (4T 653). As a result, she counseled her readers to avoid the "frivolous and excit-ing," even if such stories had religious sentiments and moral lessons appended to them (MYP 272).

On the positive side, Ellen White advocated pastimes that would utilize time wisely and help people in the formation of character (AH 417). In terms of both sports and entertainment, perhaps her most basic counsel was for people to participate in that which built them up rather than those things that merely amused or entertained or provided an escape from the realities of life. "There is," she penned, "a distinction between recreation and amusement. Recreation, when true to its name, re-creation, tends to strengthen and build up. Calling us aside from our ordinary cares and occupations, it affords refreshment for mind and body, and thus enables us to return with new vigor to the earnest work of life. Amusement, on the other hand, is sought for the sake of pleasure and is often carried to excess; it absorbs the energies that are required for useful work and thus proves to be a hindrance to life's true success" (Ed 207).

Chapter Eleven

Perspective

In this volume we have surveyed the times in which Ellen White lived, and to a lesser extent we have sampled how she responded to that world. In closing we will spend a little time analyzing her relationship to her world and her relevance to ours.

ELLEN WHITE AND HER WORLD

The most basic thing we can say about Ellen White is that she was immersed in her world; she was a nineteenth-century person who faced nineteenth-century issues with a nineteenth-century frame of reference. Even a casual acquaintance with her writings indicates that she was quite alert to her world and to the social and religious issues of her time. She not only lived in that world, but responded to it in language that her contemporaries could understand.

On the other hand, Ellen White was not a reflection of her times. In fact, she stood over against much of the "common wisdom" of her day. One has only to think of her ideas in such areas as health and education to realize that she was more in harmony with the social reformers of her times than she was with the times themselves.

But even when compared to the reformers of the late nineteenth and early twentieth centuries she had subtle and not so subtle differences. The most basic difference between Ellen White and the reformers of her day was philosophic. Every issue she dealt with she handled within the great controversy frame of reference, the galactic struggle between Christ and Satan. More specifically, she set forth her counsel for both daily life and reform in the context of the messages of the three angels of Revelation 14:6-12 and their (i.e., Adventism's) mission to a troubled world at the end of time.

Thus health reform was not an end in itself, as it was for many in the health reform movement. Rather, it was the right arm of the third angel to prepare a people for the end of time (1T 486, 559; 6T 327). In a similar manner, even though she had a burden for the poor and for helping them, she cautioned the Adventist Church away from the approach of the Salvation Army and the Social Gospel. That work was important to her, but other people were willing to do it. But no one else would preach the three angels' messages to all the world if Adventism didn't do it (8T 185; letter 3, 1900; MM 311, 312).

The screens by which she sorted out priorities were philosophic. Such criteria as the important issues in the great controversy, the unique end-time mission of the church, and so on shaped her counsel to the church. In that sense she can be said to have had a unique slant from which to advocate a reform agenda that she shared with others of her era.

Ellen White was a forceful proponent for the views that she set forth. Anyone reading her biography or the history of the Seventh-day Adventist Church will be able to see the magnitude of her impact on those around her.

ELLEN WHITE AND OUR WORLD

OK, you may be thinking, Ellen White had a message for the late nineteenth and early twentieth centuries, but does she have anything to say to us? And if so, how relevant is it?

That is an excellent question, and it comes close to the heart of the purpose for writing both *Reading Ellen White* and *Ellen*

White's World. Ellen White is relevant to our day because the is-sues she faced are perennial and because the principles she set forth to meet those issues are applicable across time and space. In other words, core issues and realities don't change all that much, even though surface manifestations do. The basic needs and prob-lems of humanity in a world of sin along with the Christian prin-ciples to fill those needs and meet those problems are universal. That is why the Bible is still a relevant book. The same holds true for Ellen White. She set forth principles that are just as valid today as they were a century ago.

But if we are going to get the most from her writings, we need to move beyond surface reading and begin to uncover the universal principles that undergird her counsel. That is where historical understanding becomes important.

Ellen White's statements consist of at least two components. The first is elements of time and place. The second is universal principles. Let's take, for example, Ellen White's counsel that we should teach every young woman "to harness and drive a horse" so that "they would be better fitted to meet the emergencies of life" (Ed 216, 217). Now, that advice doesn't appear to be very useful or meaningful to us. But that is only true at the surface level, at the level of time and place. The undergirding principle is that young women, just as young men, should be self-suffi-cient in their transportation needs. In a similar manner, Christians generally don't take off their shoes when they enter a church, as did Moses when he entered the presence of God (Ex. 3:5). That was a particular of time and place. But the principle of reverence in God's presence is universally applicable.

What history teaches us is that issues of health, civil rights, and temperance are always with us. And even though the civil rights issues before the Civil War differed from those after the war, the same principles were applicable as people faced civil rights challenges in two different eras. In fact, those principles are still valid today, even though the particular surface configura-tions of civil rights struggles have changed.

Thus we need to train ourselves to read for both the universal human issues and the timeless principles given us to meet them. That means that we need to read historically. As we read Ellen White (or the Bible) we must identify the universal principles that undergird her counsels in a given time and place. Then, through the guidance of the Holy Spirit, we need to apply those principles to our own historic time and place. As an aid in that process, an understanding of the general historical context in which Ellen White spoke is important, as is the specific context in which she counseled individuals and churches, whenever it is available.

Because of the principle-based nature of Ellen White's writings, we don't need to start from square one in thinking from a Christian perspective about such things as contemporary soap operas. Their modernness is only skin-deep. At a deeper level the same escapist and emotional dynamics operated in the nineteenth century in the form of the sentimental novel and the acted-out melodrama. The same applies to other topics that Ellen White addressed. *In actual fact the past is always with us in principle; the past is always present. That's what makes nineteenth-century or first-century counsel relevant in our day.*